Eerie ARIZONA

PATRICK WHITEHURST

*Illustrations by Jason McLean
and Paul Van De Carr*

THE
History
PRESS

Published by The History Press
Charleston, SC
www.historypress.com

Front cover: Eerie Arizona's state seal. *Illustration by Jason McLean.*

First published 2024

Manufactured in the United States

ISBN 9781467156141

Library of Congress Control Number: 2024938231

For everyone like me, fans and followers of the weird and the unexplained.

CONTENTS

CONTENTS

INTRODUCTION

Welcome to the weirdness. Have a seat and make yourself comfortable. Writing about the Grand Canyon State is like making a Sonoran hot dog. Lots of ingredients must be added before you call it done. For those who have never tried one, you're missing out. And they're a southern Arizona staple, especially in Tucson. The directions vary on how they're made, but the ingredients are the same: the hot dog is wrapped in bacon, the bolillo roll sliced to create a pocket, and tomatoes, onions, beans and sauce are drizzled on top. Some grill the bread, some add avocado, but the intent is there, no matter the variation.

Eerie Arizona is the same.

Named an official state in 1912, Arizona became known as the "five C" state for its cattle, cotton, copper, citrus and warm climate. In this book, you'll see why chupacabras could very easily make Arizona the state of the "six Cs." New residents flocked to the state in the early 1900s as result of the health benefits ascribed to warm, dry climates. This was particularly true in the southern half of Arizona. Today, Phoenix and Tucson still hold the title of the state's top two largest cities. According to the 2021 American Community Survey, Phoenix residents added 1,591,119 souls to the state's population. Tucson adds an additional 538,167 to the mix. This accounts for the sheer number of witnesses to the infamous "Phoenix lights" incident in March 1997. If an unknown group of objects was looking for secrecy, it certainly could have chosen a more secretive location anywhere else in the state.

Arizona's state flag consists of thirteen rays of red and yellow on its top half, symbolizing the Spanish conquistadors, while the star signifies the state's history with copper. *Illustration by Jason McLean.*

While Flagstaff has a much smaller population than Phoenix and Tucson, it offers features the others don't—a high elevation for one. At seven thousand feet above sea level, the Coconino County community serves as a training ground for Olympic athletes and has the distinction of being close to Grand Canyon, the state's most visited location. It was at the Grand Canyon where Glen and Bessie Hyde vanished shortly after their marriage. The two decided to spend their honeymoon shooting the rapids along the Colorado River within the canyon and quickly vanished, becoming part of one of the area's most famous missing person cases, as you'll soon learn.

Arizona wouldn't be so well known were it not also for the Wild West. Tombstone, Arizona, is another stop on the state tour and is known everywhere for one remarkable event—and it lasted only thirty seconds. The notorious Gunfight at the O.K. Corral took place in 1881 and ended up branding the community for the rest of its life. But it wasn't the only gun battle that took place there. Brutal deaths were part of the town's history, which explains why there are so many ghostly tales within the community, particularly at the old Bird Cage.

Sedona is one of the crown jewels of the state. Straddled by jaw-dropping red rock formations, the small community sits snugly between Prescott and Flagstaff at the heart of the state. In 1902, around the time the community got its first post office, tourists were visiting in droves. The area was known for its apple orchards and farmland. Today, it's known for its inspirational beauty and relaxing resorts, and it's said to be a spiritual haven for those seeking it. It's also home to the vortices, "swirling" bundles of earthly energy that many believe offer healing properties. It could be the vortices draw others to it as well, including creatures that stand nine feet tall, covered in black fur. They're not talking about bears when locals refer to these creatures—they're talking about Bigfoot. Encounters have been recorded in the red rock community as well as near Grand Canyon, as you'll read in subsequent chapters.

Arizona is indeed eerie. We wouldn't want it any other way. Like the Sonoran hot dog, it's all about the ingredients. Factor in the gorgeous weather with the deadly fires, the beauty of a lush desert landscape with the grunting Bigfoot outside your window and the world-renowned cuisine with horrifying alien abductions, and you have a meal worth savoring. As any chef worth their salt will tell you, it tastes better when made with love.

For a chaser, tequila might be best.

PART I

HISTORIC MYSTERIES

1

GRAND CANYON

Death in the Vast National Park

The Grand Canyon may be known for its geological grandeur and awe-inspiring beauty, but it's also a place where a person can go missing, never to be seen again. Not every visitor to this majestic venue returns.

The canyon sits prominently in the north of Arizona, bordering Nevada, Utah, Colorado and New Mexico. In all, the Grand Canyon spans just over 1,904 square miles and is larger than the entire state of Rhode Island. It's believed to be at least five, if not six, million years old. Formed by the Colorado River, which cuts a swath through the stone, the canyon measures 270 miles long, 18 miles across in spots and at least 1 mile deep. Six million years of river erosion have unearthed views of the oldest rocks on the planet, making the canyon a treasure trove for geologists and geology buffs. The exposed cross-sections date back, it's estimated, two billion years.

Human life within the canyon has been dated to at least twelve thousand years ago, to the age from which the earliest figurines and spear tips have been discovered. It's believed early hunters used the canyon during the last ice age. During this period, giant mammals, such as mammoths, still roamed the landscape. Among the items discovered in caves have been twig figurines depicting various animals, such as big horn sheep.

Several Native tribes have called the land in and around Grand Canyon their home, including the Navajo, Hopi, Zuni and Paiute. The Havasupai tribe can now be found within the Grand Canyon. Nearby are the famous Havasupai Falls, which continue to draw tens of thousands of visitors a year. Hopi guides led the first Europeans to the Grand Canyon as part of

Architect Mary Colter shows off blueprints in this photograph from the Grand Canyon, taken in 1935, less than ten years after the Hydes disappeared. Colter is famous at the Canyon for designing Lookout Studio, Hermit's Rest and the breathtaking Desert View Tower. *Grand Canyon National Park.*

a Spanish expedition in the 1540s. Years later, in the 1850s, a mapping expedition made their way through the area, led by Josheph Ives and geologist John Newberry. A decade later, famed explorer John Wesley Powell provided a detailed map of the Colorado River as it wound through the formidable Canyon.

By the 1800s, settlers had begun to call the area home. While these early settlers originally mined copper, their ideas for drawing in tourism dollars wasn't far behind. By the time a spur of the Santa Fe Railroad had connected to nearby Flagstaff, Arizona, to Grand Canyon Village in 1901, President Benjamin Harrison had turned the park into a national preserve.

It wasn't until 1919 that President Woodrow Wilson named the Grand Canyon a national park. The decision to do so was the result of an effort to protect the land and everything within it. The job of those who work for the National Park Service is to protect and preserve the resources located on the land. They also preserve human history on the land and its cultural impact the world over. This includes everything from protecting archaeological sites to artifacts and structures that once belonged to the area's Native inhabitants.

Later, in 1976, Grand Canyon National Park was named a World Heritage Site.

Located within the national park is a museum that contains artifacts related to the park, several retrieved from the bottom of the canyon itself. These artifacts include famous paintings, notes scrawled on paper and left in old soup cans and even passenger plane debris recovered from a 1956 midair collision. Thousands of researchers make use of the museum's vast collection annually. Museum staff have been tasked with this work since the park opened. There are more than one million items in the museum's collection, which includes archive manuscripts and history, geology, paleontology, ethnology, biology and archaeology collections.

The museum is a storage and research facility. The structure housing the artifacts, finished in 1999, comprises approximately six thousand square feet, with every inch of it climate controlled. The museum is also open to those who seek to conduct research and study. For each request—and more than two thousand requests are made every year—a staff person must be present to assist, and on-site examinations are permitted of the artifacts. Anyone hoping to view items for research or study purposes is asked to make an appointment whenever possible.

It was here that researchers made a significant discovery related to one of the most famous cold cases in Arizona's history, which this book touches on.

Park rangers with the Grand Canyon National Park routinely report on human remains found in the canyon—some discovered by *other* visitors. Sadly, many of the skeletal remains are never identified, but others are, giving the families involved a much-needed sense of closure.

The discovery of remains is a common occurrence, and each discovery is reported to the public. A 2014 report detailed unidentified remains found with abandoned camping gear near the Hermit Creek drainage. The remains were collected and sent to the Coconino County medical examiner for DNA testing. It was believed the remains were connected to the 2010 disappearance of a Tucson man. It's common for search crews, while looking for someone who's gone missing at the canyon, to discover the remains of someone else, according to a 2015 newspaper report. Remains have been discovered by hikers, river rafters and park personnel. For instance, in 2015, rafters who were searching for antique mining gear found aircraft wreckage while on a one-day expedition. Humans remains were scattered nearby.

It's not unheard of for visitors to stumble across the remains of lost hikers while exploring the rugged terrain around the Grand Canyon. *Illustration by Jason McLean.*

It's believed the plane, piloted by a missing Glendale man, may have been crashed intentionally, according to an Associated Press news article.

According to the book *Over the Edge: Death in Grand Canyon*, by Thomas M. Myers and Michael P. Ghiglieri, around 900 people are known to have perished at the canyon from a variety of causes. It's reported that just over 10 people die at Grand Canyon yearly. The top causes of death at the canyon include aerial crashes (airplanes and helicopters), falls from the cliffs, the heat and other environmental issues and drowning. Flight-related deaths at the canyon number around 380 in total, deaths from falling (either by suicide or accidental) number about 198 and environmental deaths (starvation, heat, cold, floods, lightning, etc.) number around 124. There have also been 39 known murders reported at the Grand Canyon.

It may seem out of place to discuss weddings and honeymoons in a chapter about mysterious deaths, but the two, oddly enough, go hand in hand more than one might think.

For most, honeymoons complete the wedding ritual. It's the finishing touch to an event that binds two people in holy union—or at least a legal union. Honeymoons tend to include a trip somewhere, with just the bride and groom, where they celebrate their love and plan their impending future as a married couple.

Honeymoons, historians believe, stem from an uglier period in history in which a groom would kidnap, forcibly marry and then whisk away his bride to an undisclosed location to impregnate her. This was all done for the groom to get out of paying a dowry to the family of the bride. Drinking wine allegedly played a significant role in the marriage-by-kidnapping concept. The word *honeymoon* allegedly stems from the practice of drinking fermented honey during a single moon cycle to improve one's fertility. This dates to at least the fifth century in Europe. In Nordic, the act is known as *hjunottsmanathr*.

The idea of traveling for one's honeymoon stems from a tradition started in nineteenth-century Britain. A newly married couple would visit relatives who had missed the wedding—a family tour of sorts. The idea of a honeymoon as a personal adventure for the newlyweds came later, and the concept of what a honeymoon should entail continues to evolve. It isn't all about sitting on a beach with an alcoholic beverage anymore. Many opt to make their vacations more lavish and more energetic than others.

This was certainly the case with the newly married Hyde couple. Their idea of a honeymoon included running the rapids in the Grand Canyon. That decision led to a shorter-than-expected union.

Glen and Bessie Hyde set out in 1928 to follow the Colorado River through the Grand Canyon by boat, particularly a type of craft known as a sweep scow. Glen Hyde, born in 1898, was an experienced boater. He grew up, according to family members, piloting canoes on the Skeena River in British Columbia. He also made expeditions on the Peace River in Canada and later made a trip to the Pacific Ocean with his younger sibling, Jeanne Hyde, along the Salmon River.

Bessie, born in 1905 to William and Charlotte Haley, had an eye for entertainment. She met Glen in 1927 while the two were on a boat trip to Los Angeles. The two were married in Twin Falls, Idaho, the very next year. The two decided quickly on their honeymoon plans, too. They planned to take a river trip through the Grand Canyon, utilizing Glen's boating knowledge and Bessie's status as the first woman to travel the Colorado River to gain immediate attention from the world at large, landing them interviews and book deals. There was even talk of a vaudeville play based on their adventure. The plan was for them to arrive in Needles, California, in early December. They disembarked from Green River, Utah, in late October.

The construction of their sweep scow cost fifty dollars and took a mere two days to complete. The couple named their honeymoon ride *Rain-in-the-face*. They stocked it with a bedspring, journals and various other supplies that would help them make it through a river trip of that length. Only one thing was missing: lifejackets.

Despite their lack of safety precautions, the couple embarked on their journey without incident and made it to Bright Angel Creek, where they

The Hydes, historians speculate, may have encountered rough waters while navigating the Colorado River during their honeymoon. *Illustration by Jason McLean.*

disembarked for a climb up South Kaibab Trail. Though it was only a short sojourn, the two met up with Grand Canyon icon Emery Kolb. Kolb would later recount that Bessie Hyde was ready to abandon the trip, but Glen was not. Glen got his way, and the two left the next day after Kolb gave them a brief tour of the Rim. Kolb offered them lifejackets for the remainder of the journey, which Glen declined.

When the two returned to the river, they encountered Adolph Sutro, the grandson of the famous Sutro. Glen and Adolph chatted about the scow before Adolph agreed to join the Hydes for a short trip to Hermit Trail, totaling approximately eight miles. Sutro, who hiked out as planned, was the last person to see the Hyde couple alive.

Early December fell upon Needles, California, only without Glen and Bessie. Rollin Hyde, Glen's father, knew something had happened to the newlyweds when he received no word of their safe return home. He made his way from Idaho to Las Vegas to begin a search for the couple. Within days, he had multiple search parties engaged in a hunt for the missing newlyweds. The search included trackers and aerial reconnaissance. Search planes made a discovery on December 19: a stranded boat on the river. But it was not just any boat—it was a scow. By Christmas Eve, Rollin was underway on his own craft, which had been salvaged by the Kolb brothers. The search party reached the scow by Christmas Day. The Kolb brothers, famed at the Grand Canyon for their photography, documented on film what they found.

They discovered the scow in remarkably good condition, its items still aboard. These items included Bessie's diary, a gun, food and other supplies. The Kolb brothers gathered what they could and cut the scow loose. No one could tell what had become of the boat's two human inhabitants.

Rollin went home to Idaho to mourn the loss of his son and daughter-in-law, though he did return to the canyon a year later to conduct a fruitless search for their remains. Their bodies have never officially been recovered.

Over the years, historians would guess about the fate of the Hydes. Some believe Bessie murdered Glen to escape an abusive relationship, while others think the two met their end while navigating a particularly nasty stretch of rapids.

Those who suppose Bessie survived the expedition by killing her husband have plenty of stories to back up their claim, including a tale told around a campfire in 1971 during a Grand Canyon boat tour. An elderly woman admitted to those gathered around the fire that she had indeed killed her husband and hiked out of the Grand Canyon on her own. It was said the woman bore a striking resemblance to Bessie. Her claim was never proven or disproven and is still discussed to this day.

Others believe Bessie survived the cursed honeymoon and changed her name to Georgie Clark. Clark was a well-known Grand Canyon rafter who died in 1992. It was around that time that friends began to connect the two women. Clark's colleagues, who had never been invited inside Clark's home while she was alive, began to sort through her personal belongings. They discovered items of interest, including a birth certificate that showed the name Bessie DeRoss and not Georgie Clark. A marriage license was also discovered among Georgie's items, and it was not just anyone's license—it was the license of Glen and Bessie Hyde.

The theory that Georgie was Bessie Hyde has been debunked from a handful of sources, including people who looked at photographs of the two women and determined they were not the same person. Brad Dimock, the author of *Sunk Without a Sound—The Tragic Colorado River Honeymoon of Glen and Bessie Hyde*, and Clark's biographer, Richard Westbrook, both agreed the two were not the same person.

Another theory is related to the skeletal remains found in the garage of Emery Kolb, one of the two brothers who met the Hydes on their trip.

The skeletal remains in question were discovered in 1977 upon Emery's death. Kolb's grandson Emery Lehnert made the discovery. He also found a shoe and apparel, according to a news article in the *Williams-Grand Canyon News*. A bullet hole was discovered in the skeleton's skull. Rumors began to circulate that the skull belonged to none other than Glen Hyde. This claim, while widely shared, was refuted years later when further details surfaced regarding the identity of the man whose skeleton was found in the Kolb garage, thanks to researchers with the Grand Canyon Museum Collection.

According to newspaper accounts, the remains matched the description of a body found on a ledge near Shoshone Point in June 1933. The body was discovered near a .32-caliber pistol with two remaining cartridges.

Investigators were able to match up the apparel found in both locations to determine a positive match. As mentioned previously, skeletal remains are found regularly around Grand Canyon. These discoveries are made during searches for missing persons, and in some cases, the discoveries are made by accident. One such case occurred in the summer of 2021. Crews had been dispatched to help find a Hungarian man who had gone missing that July while visiting the American Southwest.

During that effort, searchers located the remains of another missing person, fifty-six-year-old Scott Walsh, who was last seen at the South Rim in 2015, though he wasn't reported as missing at that time. According to the national park, the body had been undisturbed for a handful of years, as evidenced by the clothing, which matched the surrounding landscape, and its positioning. Walsh's body was located during an aerial search. It was spotted near the Pipe Creek overlook, about six hundred feet below the Rim. Searchers made the identification using a daypack found three miles away in 2015. Prescription medicines found in the pack were made out to Walsh, matching a driver's license found with the remains in 2021.

The missing Hungarian man's remains, meanwhile, were also discovered during the search.

A view of the Grand Canyon from 1953, taken at the South Rim near Hopi Point, illustrates the splendor and sprawl of the national park. *Grand Canyon National Park.*

Investigators believe Gabor Berczi-Tomcsanyi, who was reported missing from Las Vegas, died from a traumatic injury obtained in a fall. His vehicle was found in August 2021, a few days prior to the discovery of his remains about 430 feet below Yavapai Point.

While the discovery of human remains isn't an everyday occurrence at Grand Canyon, there is one place where it's expected. The Grand Canyon Pioneer Cemetery is located within the national park near the Shrine of the Ages. Those buried on the designated property include Ellsworth Kolb, Eddie McKee, Captain John Hance, Pete Berry and more. To be eligible for burial in the cemetery, an individual must have made a significant contribution to the park in one way or another, including efforts to develop the longevity of Grand Canyon or aid in protecting the area. To be buried here, one must also have lived in the park for three years at a minimum. All of the cemetery's final resting locations have been spoken for, according to the National Park Service.

A memorial for the victims of the 1956 airline collision can be found within the cemetery, honoring the 128 individuals who lost their lives in the sky above the canyon. The collision occurred on June 30, 1956, when a TWA Constellation plane and a United Airlines DC-7 collided over the Colorado and Little Colorado Rivers. The aircraft, which had left Los Angeles, struck at an altitude of about twenty thousand feet, becoming the worst aviation disaster in history at the time and leading to the formation of the Federal Aviation Authority (FAA).

Also among those who died in the canyon and were later buried in the cemetery is William Henery Ashurst, a Grand Canyon prospector and resident of nearby Flagstaff. Ashurst was killed in 1901, when a landslide buried him near Grand Canyon Village. John Hance, who is also buried there, was a friend of William and had him interred in the cemetery.

Surveyor Peter Hansbrough was killed on the Colorado River in 1889 while surveying for the railroad. He drowned with two others whose bodies were never located. His remains were subsequently buried at the cemetery.

Aside from the cemetery, other locations within the national park mark the final resting places of early Grand Canyon inhabitants. These past inhabitants include William Wallace Bass, whose ashes were spread over Holy Grail Temple via airplane in 1933. However, his name can be found on a marker in the cemetery beside the final resting place of his wife, Ada. Bass was an entrepreneur who developed more than fifty miles of trails within the Grand Canyon, which he used for mining and tourism purposes. He's the name behind the North and South Bass Trails at the canyon. He constructed the trails in the mid-1880s.

Rees Griffiths was killed in 1922 while working on the South Kaibab Trail. A boulder struck Griffiths following a dynamite blast near the river. His grave can still be seen in a spot near Phantom Ranch. Those who work at the ranch still tend to his grave site every year. Found within Bright Angel Canyon, Phantom Ranch is a popular spot. Located 4,600 feet below the South Rim, it's not an easy spot to get to. The complex, made up of an assortment of structures, can be reached only by boat, by foot or by mule, a popular mode of transport within the national park. Trails from the North and South Rims converge near Phantom Ranch, and two bridges span across the Colorado River nearby, making it a busy location for travelers.

In the 1920s, Grand Canyon Village's El Tovar Hotel manager Charles Brant and his wife, Olga, were buried near the hotel on a hill that looked over the village. When their dog Razzle Dazzle followed them in death in 1928, it's said the animal's remains were also buried there. That same year, John Ivens Post no. 42 erected a gate to the Pioneer Cemetery, which is still standing.

2
ROUTE 666

Cursed Highway

Hey Satan
Payin' my dues
Playin' in a rocking band

AC/DC wrote the memorable lyrics to this hit song, "Highway to Hell," for their 1979 album of the same name after touring for years. While the song refers to the rigors of the rock-and-roll lifestyle, it could be easily applied to one of America's most wicked highways, Route 666.

Highway 666 has a number of nicknames, including the "Highway to Hell." It's also known as Satan's Highway and the Devil's Highway. The twisty backroad spans approximately two hundred miles and crosses four states: Utah, Colorado, New Mexico and Arizona. The allegedly cursed highway runs from Monticello, Utah, to Gallup, New Mexico. Due to its unfortunate numerical assignment—or for more supernatural reasons—Highway 666 has a reputation for being one of the country's most haunted locations. Creepy tales surround the stretch of road like mile markers.

The highway is said to be one of the unluckiest stretches of road in the United States, with unexplained phenomena reported there regularly, including the appearance of ghosts, mystifying accidents and, of course, devilry from Satan himself. This includes reports of hell hound sightings and encounters with Satan's very own sedan. Other unexplained phenomena include a haunted truck, a female apparition in a white dress, skinwalkers (which are also discussed in this book), drivers who vanish without a trace and an assortment of weird lights.

Road signs for State Route 666, also known as the Devil's Highway, have been known to pop up for sale on eBay and other websites. Route 666 has since been renamed. *Public domain.*

Of course, the road itself predates the famed AC/DC song, and its name has since been changed to a moniker with less satanic connotations. The road has been around longer than Arizona has been a state, in fact. While Arizona became the nation's forty-eighth state on Valentine's Day, February 14, 1912, Route 666 has been around since at least 1848, when it served as a trading route during the Mexican-American War. It was one of Mexico's primary trading routes. Back then, it was called the Old Spanish Trail.

The two-hundred-mile drive became known as United States Route 666 in 1925. Route 666 got its name from the historic Route 66 highway, with which most Americans are familiar. Route 66 starts in Los Angeles, California, and runs more than two thousand miles to Chicago. Established in 1926, Route 66 follows a winding path across the United States, over old trails and railroad lines. The fully paved road—at least by the 1930s anyway—became known for its direct route to the West Coast. Route 66 became part of the national highway system that connected hundreds of once-remote small towns to a bustling artery of American commerce. The road remained in heavy use until 1985, when the last Route 66 town was bypassed by Interstate 40. That town, Williams, is located in northern Arizona, approximately forty miles west of Flagstaff. Route 66 was so popular among travelers that it inspired a hit television series, *Route 66*, which ran for four seasons on CBS between 1960 and 1964. All 116 episodes of the hit show were filmed on location throughout the country, in both an episodic and standalone format that featured a small cast of recurring characters. Another reason the stretch of highway remains famous today is the iconic song "(Get Your Kicks on) Route 66," sung by

Bobby Troup. Troup composed the music in 1946. The song, considered a rhythm and blues standard, is said to have been thought up by Troup on a long road trip from Pennsylvania to California.

> *If you ever plan to motor west*
> *Travel my way, that's the highway that's the best*
> *Get your kicks on Route 66.*
> *It winds from Chicago to L.A.*
> *More than 2,000 miles all the way*
> *Get your kicks on Route 66*

Troup credited his ex-wife, Cynthia, for helping him produce these quoted lyrics for the song. She traveled west with him on that road trip. While those lyrics paint the famed route in a joyful, adventurous light, Route 666 has had a far from happy history.

Part of these beliefs stem from Native legends, such as the Navajo skinwalkers. Skinwalkers are shape-shifters that can transform into various creatures, including wolves, coyotes and more. These creatures are rumored to have appeared on occasion along Route 666, including directly in front of oncoming vehicles, leaving deadly results in their wake. Portions of the roadway pass remarkably close to Native landmarks, including Shiprock in New Mexico and Ute Mountain in Colorado. These sights are considered sacred. Shiprock, called Tsé Bit'a'í in Navajo, or "rock with wings," is thought to represent a massive bird that transported the Navajo people to their home. Entry to the peak is forbidden, as the Navajo do not wish to disturb the spirits of their ancestors. The mountain is part of the Navajo Nation in San Juan County, New Mexico. It rises to an elevation just above seven thousand feet. The moniker "Shiprock" dates to the late 1800s and references the peak's resemblance to a nineteenth-century clipper ship.

While climbing Shiprock is not allowed, this has not deterred a few daredevils from doing just that. The ascent was banned for tourists in 1970, following an accident on the peak that seriously injured three climbers. Permits are issued to those who wish to hike and climb national monuments, but Shiprock is not one of them. The geology of the mountain is believed to be twenty-seven million years old.

Ute Mountain, near the Four Corners region of Colorado, is home to the Ute Mountain tribe, a part of the Ute Nation. Ute Mountain refers to the peak of the mountain range. That peak is sometimes called Sleeping Ute as well. It's named for its resemblance to a sleeping Ute chief, reclined on his back and recovering from wounds received in a great battle with "the evil ones." The site is considered a sacred Ute location to this day.

While skinwalkers are believed to inhabit portions of Route 666, hounds of hell are also said to roam there. Reports over the road's sordid history have cited claims of giant hounds chasing vehicles and managing to keep pace with the fleeing inhabitants no matter how fast they drive. The common belief is that these creatures are none other than the hounds that stand guard over the entrance to Satan's realm. They're not stopping people from entering the underworld, but they are on constant alert for those trying to escape hell.

Some, however, believe there is only one creature on the roadway, and that is Cerberus, the three-headed hound of Greek mythology. Each head on the hound's massive shoulders represents a different aspect in time: the past, present and future. The creature is said to have a serpentine tail and is often described as being covered in snakes, which appear from its body like sweat.

In English folklore, eerie black dogs with glowing red or yellow eyes are said to be agents of the devil and a harbinger of death. So popular was this belief that Sherlock Holmes author Sir Arthur Conan Doyle wrote about the dogs in his Holmes tale "The Hound of the Baskervilles." The hounds' origins could very well be found in Celtic beliefs and also Greek stories, carried over to more recent bits of British folklore. Legends of gory hell hounds exist in nearly every culture, including those in Latin America, where black dogs are said to roam the roadways, some benevolent and others malignant. This is the case with the spirit dogs, or *cadejo*, from Central American folklore. White cadejo assist weary travelers, while black cadejo are considered evil and are the sort one would not want to see on the roadway—especially not on Highway 666.

But what exactly makes the three sixes a number to fear?

The numerical designation stems from the Bible, particularly Revelation 13:18, which states:

> *Let him who has understanding calculate the number of the beast, for it is the number of man: his number is 666.*

Oddly enough, this stretch of supernatural roadway isn't the only Route 666 on the planet. In Poland, near the aptly named community of Hel, there is another Route 666. Hel, a resort community in northern Poland, was accessible by Bus Route 666. Due to the name of its destination, drivers

The mythical being Cerberus guards the gates of hell just off Route 666 and will use all three of its heads to bring fresh faces into the underworld. *Illustration by Paul Van de Carr.*

found the road's numerical designation quite apt indeed—only those who thought so were English-speaking visitors to the community, not locals. In Polish, the word for hell is *pieklo*.

Efforts by religious leaders helped change the name of the bus route in 2023, flipping the final 6 upside down and subsequently turning it into a 9, thereby removing the number of the beast from the town of Hel, at least when it comes to the designation used by PKS Gdynia, the bus operator. Despite Hel's affiliations with Satanic words, the community is known predominantly known for its pine forests and sandy beaches.

While fast car enthusiasts have gotten their kicks on Route 66, less are inclined to take their risks on Route 666. The road consists of steep elevation changes and sharp curves, which have led to a number of fatal accidents over the course of the road's existence, particularly along its New Mexico section. Route 666 features approximately four hundred dramatic turns within a sixty-mile radius alone. America's satanic designation, meanwhile, officially reached the end of the road on May 31, 2003, when government officials renamed the last segments of the road U.S. 491, which is a spur of U.S. 191, effectively putting the Devil's Highway out to pasture. Before the road was renamed, however, collectors grabbed as many of its old signs as they could, often from the side of the road itself, and the collector's items are said to have popped up for sale on eBay at the time. Aside from its new name, the road has also undergone improvements. Sections that once had just two lanes now have four, which have decreased the number of fatalities on the road.

The roadway has become so infamous that a movie was made about it in 2001. Called simply *Route 666*, the film starred Lou Diamond Phillips and Lori Petty, who played two Federal Bureau of Investigations agents delivering a mob informer to court. When they use Route 666 to elude the mob hitmen, things worsen for the FBI agents and their informant. Prior to the Lions Gate Home Entertainment movie, the roadway was also noted, briefly, in the Oliver Stone movie *Natural Born Killers*.

Mechanical issues are said to be a common occurrence along Route 666, leading believers to contend that the cause stems not from forgetting to put in oil but from the cursed stretch of asphalt itself. Everything from flat tires to inoperable engines have been seen along the side of the road. These technical matters pale in comparison to reports of the supernatural, however. A haunted semitruck is thought to cruise Route 666, seeking to

Watch out for Satan's sedan, also rumored to haunt Route 666, and be careful he doesn't drive up behind you with his brights on and ram into you. *Illustration by Jason McLean.*

ram unwitting travelers and do far worse damage than simply flatten a tire. Reports include drivers being run off the road and followed for miles by the dark vehicle.

Over the years, these tales evolved into the tale of the mad trucker of Route 666, with drivers who have cruised along the roadway, both before and after its name was changed, relaying stories of a maniacal trucker encounters. The legends start off with a lone traveler driving at night who is confronted by the terrible truck. Accounts have claimed the truck is surrounded by flame, as if it was discharged straight from the mouth of hell. Speculation abounds that the truck may belong to a real individual, a serial killer who uses a vehicle to kill, rather than an otherworldly demon.

Whether the mad trucker of Route 666 is a demon or simply a human with ill intent, their legend is shared regularly among travelers of the Devil's Highway. Satan's sedan would be a close second, as the two legends are often confused. The Satan's sedan, a vehicle black as night, uses the cover of darkness to approach travelers past sunset, blinding their rear-view mirrors with its headlights while trying to ram them from behind. According to reports, the victims pull off to the side of the road, only to discover there was never another vehicle at all.

3

PHOENIX

Hogan's Hero

We turn from the hounds of hell to a town as hot as Hades itself. Scottsdale, a swanky town in the Phoenix metropolitan area, is home to, as of 2023, a population of nearly 250,000. Today, the community is known for its restaurants and art galleries. It's also the site of one of the state's most infamous murders—a murder that's never been officially solved.

But to go there, we must first make our way east.

The town of Waterbury, Connecticut, is located on the Naugatuck River, approximately seventy-five miles northeast of New York City. In 2020, the United State census counted 114,403 residents in the city. It's the tenth-largest city in the New York metro area. Known for its industrial roots, including the production of brass castings, Waterbury is nicknamed Brass City. Time keepers, namely clocks and watches, have also become synonymous with the city's name.

Several interesting people have been born in Waterbury over the years, including famed photographer Annie Leibovitz, born in 1949; NFL player Fritz Barzilauskas; television personality Joe Cipriano; and wrestling personalities Justin Credible and Velvet Sky, among others.

Iconic actor Bob Crane was also born there on July 13, 1928, though he spent his childhood years in Stamford and ended up in Arizona many years later. Crane, the youngest of two boys, was born to Rose and Alfred Crane. While he would go on to become a television icon, his interests originally dwelled in the world of music. At eleven, he began playing the drums and went on to join the local Stamford High School orchestra, as well as its marching band. Not only did he play in his high school orchestra, but he also took part in the youth orchestra program for the Connecticut and Norwalk Symphony Orchestras. Crane graduated in 1946 and joined the national guard. According to rumors, Crane was let go from the Connecticut Symphony Orchestra after his second year due to some tomfoolery he pulled during a Bach fugue.

In 1949, Crane married his high school girlfriend, Anne Terzian. The two would go on to have three children: Karen Leslie, Robert David and Deborah Ann.

He brought his love of music with him when he accepted a job in radio for WLEA in Hornell, New York, in 1950. He would go on to work for other stations, building his name recognition along the way. By 1956, his popularity had landed him a position with CBS Radio that sent him west to Los Angeles, California. He wasted no time booking a plethora of famous names. Personalities such as Bob Hope, Frank Sinatra, Charlton Heston and even Marilyn Monroe appeared on his radio program.

Along the way, he became known as "King of the Los Angeles Airwaves." And since Crane had dashing good looks, it wasn't long before his face, not just his voice, became familiar to audiences.

Crane got his start on television soon after writer Carl Reiner appeared on his radio program. With Reiner's encouragement (or Crane's persistence), the radio host, in 1961, landed a cameo spot on *The Dick Van Dyke Show* and then an ongoing gig as dentist Dr. Dave Kelsey on *The Donna Reed Show*. His was certainly a rising star.

Crane's agent then sent him a script for a show, *Hogan's Heroes*, a sitcom, of all things, surrounding a German prisoner-of-war camp, with costars John Banner, who played Sergeant Schultz; Werner Klemperer, who played Colonel Klink; Robert Clary, who played Corporal LeBeau; and many others. They helped shape the popular series, which lasted an admirable six seasons on CBS. The program, a situational comedy set in a World War II's Stalag 13, had what seemed an odd plot for a comedy show. Nonetheless, *Hogan's Heroes* proved to be a popular program among viewers when its first episode aired in September 1965. During its run, the show earned more than ten Emmy nominations. Klemperer won two awards for his portrayal of Klink. Oddly enough, many of the actors who played Germans on the show were Jewish Holocaust survivors.

The program was both applauded and derided by critics and fans; some believed *Hogan's Heroes* served as an example of desensitization for American audiences. Fans of the show, however, considered it the height of comedy.

Behind the scenes, however, Crane was known as a man with a high sex drive. He had many sexual encounters over the years, including some with his female castmates on the show, and he was said to take photographs of and even film his exploits. Around 1970, after his divorce from Terzian, he married fellow cast member Patricia Olson, who played German secretary Helga after actor Cynthia Lynn left the role. When word of Crane's penchant for bedroom antics began to spread in Hollywood and through the tabloids, though a select few of his friends were already aware, his career suffered. Relatives and others close to the Crane family have indicated Crane's sexual appetite never veered into the illegal territory and said that it should be considered a small part of his overall life story. Nonetheless, Crane found it difficult to find work after *Hogan's Heroes* ended its run. He began to work at dinner theaters to make ends meet and made guest appearances on various television programs like *The Love Boat*.

Crane moved to Phoenix amid talk of a divorce from Olson and began to contemplate making changes to his life, which included cutting his ties with John Henry Carpenter, a close friend who helped Crane acquire video equipment at a time when such things were tough to come by. (This equipment was allegedly used to film his carnal appetites.) Crane then bought the rights to a play and hoped to see his star rise again.

Unfortunately, Crane did not live to enjoy the continued interest *Hogan's Heroes* held for fans. He was found murdered on June 29, 1978, in Scottsdale, in a first-floor unit at the Winfield Apartments. Crane, then aged forty-nine, was discovered shirtless with cuts just over his left ear and an electrical cord wrapped around his neck. When police first arrived at the scene of the crime, they found a very bloody spectacle, with blood on the walls and ceiling. They were unable to immediately identify the victim. They did, however, learn the apartment was leased to the Windmill Dinner Theatre and identified Crane with the assistance of Ed Beck, the manager of the theater. Shortly thereafter, Crane's son Robert, business manager Lloyd Vaughn and attorney Bill Goldstein were all brought to the site of the murder. Robert Crane later said he believed their arrival compromised the crime scene, according to a 2019 *Entertainment Weekly* story by Lynette Rice. Robert indicated they were allowed to touch and stroll through the apartment at will, thereby adding their presence to an active crime scene. One of the investigators that day, Detective Barry Vassal, denied the location was compromised by their presence, however.

Investigators had their sights on a prime suspect, Carpenter, as the two were alleged to have had an argument the night before Crane's body

There has never been a conviction in the Bob Crane murder case, which occurred in Scottsdale in June 1978. Crane, star of the popular television program *Hogan's Heroes*, was forty-nine years old at the time of his death. *Illustration by Jason McLean.*

was discovered. Other witnesses later came forward to claim the two did indeed have dinner that night but said there was no argument between the two. There was also no indication that the murderer had forced their way into the apartment, which led authorities to believe the killer was known to the victim. The most damning evidence came when police examined Carpenter's rental car and found traces of blood. The blood found in the car matched Crane's blood type. Despite this, the county attorney refused to issue an arrest warrant due to the lack of a murder weapon. The case remained unsolved for twelve years until another detective, Jim Raines, found a photograph that allegedly included brain tissue that was found at the time of the murder. The photograph was allowed into evidence all those years later, and in 1992, Carpenter was formally charged with Bob Crane's murder. Without sufficient evidence, however, the case still wouldn't stick. Carpenter was acquitted of the murder in 1994. He died four years later with many believing he was guilty of Crane's murder. During the court proceedings, however, speculation ran wild that, due to Crane's sexual exploits, his murderer could have been anyone from a jilted lover to the husband of a lover. It is even suggested Olson may have had something to do with Crane's death, since she would have received less money from Crane after a divorce.

There still has not been a conviction in the case.

Crane's sordid story and Hollywood fame have been written about extensively and even turned into entertainment, such as the film *Auto Focus*, which is centered on Crane's relationships and starred Greg Kinnear as Crane himself, Maria Bello as Olson and Willem Dafoe as Carpenter. Family members later said the film played up sexual angles and didn't correctly portray Crane as an actor and father.

Many of Crane's *Hogan's Heroes* costars made their way to Westwood, California, for Crane's somber funeral at St. Paul the Apostle Church. Hollywood elite, such as Patty Duke, Carroll O'Connor and John Astin, also attended. Altogether, more than 150 people turned out for the service. Robert Clary, the last of the original cast of characters, passed away in 2022. He was ninety-six.

Crane's story didn't end with his star-studded funeral. Years after Crane's death, his family members have continued to squabble among themselves. Olson, it was revealed, even went as far as to move her husband's body from its original plot and failed to inform the rest of Crane's family about the relocation, according to an *Entertainment Weekly* story. It's said she even sold Crane's "adult" films through a memorial website. The site has been shut down, and according to family members, Crane's collection of sexual photographs and videos has now been destroyed.

Hogan's Heroes remains a popular program on television channels such as MeTV, with reruns still being aired. In 2019, talk of a revival show began to circulate. Deadline.com reported in 2019 that a reboot was in the works through Village Roadshow Entertainment Group and Rough Pictures. Hints indicated the new show would feature descendants of the original cast of characters.

4

TUCSON

The Wishing Shrine Curse

Two hours or so south of Scottsdale, we find the site of another murder, though this one is said to have occurred long ago in Tucson.

Tucson's El Tirodito, commonly referred to as the Wishing Shrine, is located in a quiet spot close to the heavily populated downtown area. Tirodito, meaning "castaway" in English, can be found near 418 South Main Avenue near Tucson's downtown area. Public hours for the shrine are 6:00 a.m. and 10:30 p.m., seven days a week. The park is also known as the Rosendo S. Perez Park, named in honor of Rosendo Perez, who helped in the effort to get the Wishing Shrine officially listed in the National Register of Historic Places. Annie Laos is also credited with her efforts to get the shrine on the register. The register, for those curious, is a list of officially recognized locations that are deemed worthy of preservation. The register itself was officially authorized in 1966 by the Historic Preservation Act and created a national program to oversee public and private efforts to protect the country's historic and archaeological resources. Tucson's Wishing Shrine, which was listed in the register in 1988, is also the only shrine dedicated to a sinner. The rest are dedicated to saints.

Said to have been opened to the public around 1871, the 21,870-square-foot landmark can be found in the Old Barrio area of downtown Tucson, which is also known as Barrio Viejo, approximately sixty miles from the United States–Mexico border. The shrine was moved from its original location, and in 1928, it was located near the corner of Simpson and Main Streets just before it was moved again. The entire Tucson community is known for its rich Latino heritage, from its architecture to its cuisine. Barrio Viejo is Spanish for "old neighborhood," which makes sense since the area dates to the 1800s. The community is made up of colorful, historic adobe structures and features restaurants and breweries. Locals and visitors can be seen walking through the historic neighborhood, admiring the homes as well as the beautiful murals visible throughout the community.

In the 1970s, Barrio Viejo residents were displaced when the construction of the nearby convention center wiped out approximately eighty acres of land. All told, more than seven hundred residents were displaced. Gentrification has been an ongoing issue within the neighborhood since then, and today, homes in the region fetch a pretty penny on the real estate market. The area is still known for its diversity, however, as it dates to a time when workers from the Southern Pacific Railroad called the community home. These settlers hailed from a variety of regions, such as Europe, Asia, Africa and elsewhere. Other popular locations in the neighborhood include the Jewish History Museum and Teatro Carmen, formerly a Latin theater, which is now closed to the public. In its day, the site served as a cultural center for Barrio Viejo residents.

The shrine, as one of the most popular stops in the neighborhood, is credited with stopping the development of a proposed freeway, which was originally set to cut a swath through the Barrio.

A sign at the entrance to the small shrine states its status as a Tucson Historical Site, and a sign notifying the public that reservations must be made with the city to use the location as a wedding venue or for a large gathering is plainly visible.

El Tirodito is often adorned with wishes, which take the form of candles left to melt away, bundles of flowers and solitary offerings such as notes stuck into the crumbling shrine's brick walls and toys. Those who visit the shrine are cautioned to be wary of the reasons for making a wish at the site. The area is said to come with a curse for those who make a wish with malice in their heart. Those with forgiveness in their heart may have their wishes granted. If you light a candle and it stays burning all night, according to legend, that may also be an indicator your wish will be granted.

The shrine's story is a tragic tale, though there are variations on the story itself. The first concerns a deadly love triangle, in which an angered husband murdered the man his wife had fallen in love with. The murdered man, according to the story, died a sinner and could not be buried in a consecrated cemetery, a space formally declared to hold a divine or religious purpose.

At the Wishing Shrine in Tucson, it's said a candle that burns through the night will bestow good luck on the person who lit it. *Illustration by Jason McLean.*

True believers think the Wishing Shrine was built in 1870 on the exact spot where the man was killed. At the time, candles were lit and prayers were offered there in the hopes that the man's soul would be guided through the gates of heaven.

The most common version of the tale of forbidden love gives the sinful young man a name and age: Juan, an eighteen-year-old ranch hand. Juan, who, according to legend, married the rancher's daughter, was accused of having a sordid affair with his mother-in-law and was subsequently murdered when her husband learned of the tryst. The story states the rancher, after catching the two in bed, murdered the younger man with a hatchet. El Tirodito is his burial site.

Eighteen-year-old ranch hand Juan was caught in bed with the rancher's wife. Her husband chased him down with an axe and murdered him—or so the story goes. *Illustration by Jason McLean.*

A second story, written about in the book *Paranormal Arizona*, by Renee Harper, features a young man who had fallen in love with a beautiful young lady, but because he was a painfully shy person by nature, he never approached her. He observed, lovestruck, from afar for months and even years. When he mustered the courage to ask her parents for her hand in marriage, he learned he was too late. She'd been promised to another. Suffering from a broken heart, the young man took a gun and ended his own life. Certain believers say the shrine was erected for him, with the lit candles serving to guide him to heaven.

Another legend from Mexico opens on a young man's mother lying on her deathbed. Just before passing away, she imparts her dying wish to her son. She bade him to meet his father, whom the young man had never met before. The father, she said, then lived in Tucson. The young man traveled there and went door to door in search of his relative. When he finally got to the right house and learned his father did indeed live there, he discovered that his father was married to a young woman. She invited the young man in to wait for his father, who was out. But when the young man's father arrived home and saw the two together, he misinterpreted the situation, thinking his son was a suitor out to steal his wife from under his nose. The father flew into a rage and murdered the young man with an axe, like the common story of Juan Oliveras, only to learn of his mistake later.

Leaving Tucson for the moment, let's look at another popular community in the northern half of the state, one known for a different kind of magic.

5
SEDONA

Vortexes

Sedona is a community of approximately ten thousand individuals, according to the 2020 United States census. Situated in red rock country, the community can be found along State Route 89A between Flagstaff and Cottonwood. The Village of Oak Creek is often considered a part of the larger Sedona community due to their proximity to each other, though the Village of Oak Creek is closer to Interstate 17 than Sedona. The red rocks surrounding Sedona are 350 million years old and have been home to Native tribes, including the Sinagua, for approximately 1,000 years. The Yavapai consider the land sacred but not for any metaphysical reason. Many of their creation stories spring from the Verde Valley among the red rocks. They were forced to abandon their home in 1875 during the Great Exodus. The Yavapai people hold a gathering in the area each February to honor the event.

Western settlers arrived in the Sedona area around 1876. Included among the handful of early settlers was J.J. Thompson, who staked out a plot of land thanks to the Homestead Act of 1862. Thompson claimed his chunk of property in 1876 and built a log cabin across from the modern-day Indian Gardens Store, which, of course, didn't exist back then. What did exist were the remains of an actual garden made by the Natives who once lived there. Thanks to a nearby spring, Thompson found the location's conditions perfect for his new life and new land, which he called Indian Gardens. Others eventually made their way to the region, where they created irrigation canals and brought along horses, cattle and other livestock. With the help of the canals, orchards soon became a fixture in the area.

Bell Rock is visible in this photograph from 2002. Located between Sedona and the Village of Oak Creek, Bell Rock is considered one of the area's popular vortex sites. *National Archives and Records Administration.*

Farmer Frank Pendley is known as one of Oak Creek's more memorable early settlers due to his engineering skills, particularly his understanding of irrigation. The apples and pears grown from his expertise were sold throughout the Verde Valley and beyond, even as far west as Los Angeles. Pendley staked out his homestead near what is today Slide Rock State Park. His irrigation system can be found there, still in use.

Sedona got its name from Sedona Schnebly, who, along with her husband, T.C., moved west from Missouri and opened a hotel and general store there. They were among the first fifteen or so homesteaders to call the locality home. When T.C. opened the first post office in the community, it was said he needed to produce a one-word name for the town. So, his brother Ellsworth suggested he name the town after his wife. Sedona Schnebly was born in Missouri on February 24, 1877, little realizing she would go down in history. Her father named her Sedona because he liked the way it sounded. According to the Sedona Heritage Museum, her name is original and doesn't hail from Spain or have Native origins.

Sedona, as anyone who's lived there can tell you, is a place of wonder and mysticism. It's said the entirety of Sedona rests on top of a sacred place. These sacred places in Sedona are known as vortexes, or vortices. A vortex— and there are actual sites in the Sedona area that are allegedly intensified points—are centers of mystical energy that offer healing and, even more beneficial to some, meditative energies. The most popular vortexes in Sedona include Bell Rock, Cathedral Rock, Boynton Canyon and Airport Mesa. Each site is believed to radiate energy, emanating special attributes, such as healing energies, rejuvenation and more. Other sites include a vortex on Schnebly Hill Road, the Chapel of the Holy Cross and Courthouse Butte.

New Age historians say the area grew into its metaphysical roots in the 1950s, when local women hosted spiritual events in their houses. It's said a number of the vortex locations, labeled with magnetic, electromagnetic or electric energy, were identified by a psychic channeler named Page Bryant.

Visitors flock to Sedona for these sites, and on any given day, they can be seen meditating or doing yoga at the intensified vortex sites. Tour companies offer visitors the opportunity to explore the vortex sites, and metaphysical and spiritual shops that sell crystals and more can be found throughout the area.

Subtle sensations have been reported at vortexes, from electromagnetic pulls to the more subtle feeling of vibrations and tingles. Others simply call it a "vibe." There are a variety of ways in which the vortexes are believed to interact with the human body, and healers believe they're a profound source of reviving energy, which, when channeled correctly, can restore a person's balance, both physically and spiritually. Vortex healing, it's believed, can remove negative sensibilities, emotions and more.

Bell Rock, an electric vortex, is located north of the village of Oak Creek, a Sedona bedroom community of sorts, and reaches an elevation of 4,919 feet at its summit. It was formed out of horizontally bedded sedimentary rock of the Permian Supai Foundation, a section of red bed deposits found in the Colorado Plateau. The Supai Group consists of sandstone and sandy shale red beds. The strongest vortex vibrations, according to Thrillist.com, come from the region's north side.

Cathedral Rock, another vortex site, is located in the Coconino National Forest but not in Coconino County itself, as a portion of the Sedona area sits in two counties: Coconino County and Yavapai County. This natural sandstone butte, located in Yavapai County, is one of the most photographed sights in the state. Found about two miles from uptown Sedona, it has an elevation, at its peak, of 4,967 feet. The most common access point to this vortex is United States Forest Service Trail no. 170.

The Boynton Canyon Vortex, an electromagnetic vortex, can be reached via the Boynton Canyon Trail no. 47, which offers visitors a paved parking lot. The area, also known as the Kachina Woman Vortex, is referred to as a box canyon, or a narrow passage with high, vertical walls and a flat walking area. The area is the spiritual home of the Yavapai Apache

Yoga, meditation and other holistic pursuits are practiced in Sedona, particularly at the vortex sites. While there are other such locations in Sedona, the entire city is thought to emit special energies. *Illustration by Jason McLean.*

tribe. The canyon is located approximately two miles west of Sedona off Dry Creek Road. As of 2024, a park pass is required to park at the paved lot, but it is considered an easy hike for those who wish to visit a vortex without breaking a sweat.

The Airport Mesa Vortex is also easy to reach, as it is smack dab in the middle of town. The area can be accessed by the Airport Loop/Tabletop Trails nos. 211 and 212, which circle the mesa, and it is, obviously, conveniently located near the Sedona Airport. Parking is also available here. The hike offers spectacular views of the Sedona region, including views of Bell Rock, Coffee Pot Rock and other highlights. The energy that is emitted from this vortex is said to have rejuvenating qualities. Visitors to Airport Mesa have also claimed to see colored orbs floating through the air. What those orbs may be is anyone's guess. Experts believe different colored orbs have different spiritual meanings, like blue represents healing and green represents growth.

The vortex area along Schnebly Hill Road can be accessed by Forest Service Trail no. 158, which climbs up Schnebly Hill just past the Oak Creek Bridge along State Route 179. Four-wheel drive vehicles are recommended for Schnebly Hill Road. Bicycles are also allowed on this stretch but are prohibited in wilderness or offroad areas. Drones are prohibited in the area's wilderness. This vortex, like Airport Mesa, is known for its views of the surrounding areas, including Munds Mountain, Bear Wallow Canyon and, of course, the area's plentiful red rock formations.

Chapel of the Holy Cross is located at 780 Chapel Road in Sedona. The church, built in 1956, is open seven days a week from 9:00 a.m. to 5:00 p.m. Some visitors make the pilgrimage to this area because of the vortex said to be located there, but others come to admire the breathtaking church found in the Coconino National Forest. Senator Barry Goldwater, at the time the church was built, approved a special-use permit that allowed the church to be constructed. The chapel was originally commissioned by Sedona rancher Marguerite Brunswig Staude.

According to the church's website, chapeloftheholycross.com, more than one miracle has been reported at the church, whether from divine intervention or the mysterious energy of the vortex. One woman from Atlanta said the church answered her prayers for a new kidney after she visited the area with her husband. In the past, she'd missed getting a new kidney, but hours after visiting the chapel, she was informed that one was finally waiting for her. A three-day candle she had lit, according to the story, went out the moment her successful operation ended. Another story concerns a woman who visited the church after deciding to discontinue her treatment for cancer following years of procedures and chemotherapy. After visiting the church, she opted for one more treatment but then decided to listen to the words of God that she'd heard during her trip to the chapel. She hasn't looked back, and a decade later, she wrote in a statement, she continues to thrive.

The Courthouse Butte area, which contains a magnetic vortex, is located within Yavapai County near the Village of Oak Creek. With a summit at 5,454 feet, this vortex site is close to the Bell Rock Vortex. It's made up of horizontally bedded sedimentary rock of the Permian Supai Formation. A butte is defined as a solitary hill with vertical cliffs and an often flat top. They're typically smaller in size than mesas or plateaus. A moderate four-mile hike circles the location.

Books and information on the vortexes can be found everywhere in the Sedona community. The area's gift shops offer an array of choices for those seeking to learn more about the vortexes, with energy workers claiming it's not just the sites previously listed that offer mysterious beacons of energy but the entire Sedona community.

As anyone who's visited the town can attest, it certainly has its charms.

PART II

HAUNTED PLACES

6

GRAND CANYON

El Tovar Haunts

While Sedona is known for its natural beauty, the land north of there, particularly the Grand Canyon, is as well—more so, in fact, as its natural appeal has no comparison. It's a no brainer that the Grand Canyon is a wonder. Its views are often life-changing for those who see it for the first time. The vast sight has inspired poetry, music and art and is one of the natural wonders of the world.

It's also home to ghostly phenomena of all shapes and sizes, including the historic El Tovar, which we'll get into shortly.

A natural wonder is defined by its breathtaking organic splendor. There are seven natural wonders in the world: the Northern Lights, the Grand Canyon, Parícutin, Mount Everest, Harbor of Rio de Janeiro, Victoria Falls and the Great Barrier Reef. The Northern Lights, found in the Northern Hemisphere, are a dazzling combination of dancing lights seen best in the night sky. These lights intensify as one heads north, toward the Arctic Pole. The best spots to view the northern lights include northern Canada, Alaska, Iceland, Norway, Sweden and Finland. The Grand Canyon's esteemed position is obvious considering its sheer size and breathtaking grandeur. Parícutin, named a natural wonder in 1997, is a cinder cone volcano in Mexico in the state of Michoacan. The volcano, now dormant, surged in 1943 and formed over a nine-year period. With its distinction as the tallest mountain in the world, standing more than 8,800 feet above sea level, Mount Everest also makes the list of natural wonders. Located in Asia, Everest's summit stands between the borders of China and Nepal. The Harbor of

Rio de Janeiro, also known as Guanabara Bay, is found along the coast of Brazil. As the world's largest bay, it boasts a circumference of 31 miles and depths from 16 feet to 130 feet. Found between Zimbabwe and Zambia on the African continent, Victoria Falls makes up the world's largest "sheet of falling water." The falls are an impressive 354 feet tall, which is quite a feat for the widest group of waterfalls in the world. The Great Barrier Reef, located off the coast of Australia, is the world's largest coral reef chain. The reef is composed of nearly three thousand individual reefs and covers 345,000 square miles.

The seven wonders of the world, on the other hand, are filled with humanity's remarkable architectural and engineering accomplishments. While the original seven wonders of the ancient world were selected by Greek historians, modern lists have been compiled to recognize extraordinary structures from various periods and regions.

Manufactured worldly wonders are numerous, from structures built in ancient times to more modern endeavors. Egypt's Great Pyramid of Giza, constructed around 2,560 BCE during the reign of Pharaoh Khufu for his personal use after death, is one of the world's monumental ancient wonders. It's the largest and oldest of the three pyramids in Giza. Another wonder of the ancient world is Egypt's Lighthouse of Alexandria, known as the Pharos of Alexandria, which was constructed on the island of Pharos in the third century BCE and guided ships to the Port of Alexandria. Iraq's alleged Hanging Gardens of Babylon were said to be a lush oasis of plants and trees built on terraces at Babylon. Philo of Byzantium and Strabo described the hanging gardens as a lush oasis of plants and trees constructed on terraces overlooking the city of Babylon. Greece's statue of Zeus in Olympia was crafted by famed sculptor Phidias sometime around 435 BCE. The statue of Zeus showed the Greek god seated on his throne, dripping with gold and ivory embellishments. It's thought to have once stood in Olympia's Temple of Zeus. Greece also hosted the massive bronze statue called Colossus of Rhodes on the Greek island of Rhodes. Skillfully made around 280 BCE, the Colossus was a massive bronze statue of the sun god Helios, and it is believed to have fallen due to an earthquake. Turkey's immense Temple of Artemis at Ephesus was dedicated to the Greek goddess Artemis and was rebuilt multiple times, though it's estimated to have finally been destroyed in 401 CE. Turkey is also home to the Mausoleum at Halicarnassus, built in the fourth century BCE as a 148-foot-tall tomb for the ruler of Caria, Mausolus.

An international poll conducted in 2007 by the New7Wonders Foundation created a list of modern wonders from diverse cultures and varying periods.

The New7Wonders were chosen by public voting and expert opinion. At the top of that list is the Great Wall of China. Covering more than thirteen thousand miles, the Great Wall was originally built to protect China from its many invaders; today, it draws sightseers from all over the world. Jordan's Petra can be found carved into the cliffs in the southern region of the country. The rock-cut site was the capital of the Nabatean Kingdom in the fourth century BCE. Another astounding marvel is Brazil's Christ the Redeemer, which stands atop the Corcovado Mountain in Rio de Janeiro, Brazil. The religious statue is a symbol of Christianity and a local Brazilian icon. The grand statue overlooks the city with outstretched arms. In Peru, Machu Picchu was built in the fifteenth century by the Incas. The citadel is nestled in the Andes Mountains and is one of the most visited archaeological sites in the world. Mexico's Chichen Itza is located on the Yucatan Peninsula and was a major city of the Mayan civilization. Its most famous structure, the Pyramid of Kukulkan, aligns with the sun's movements during equinoxes. Italy's Roman Colosseum, built in the first century CE, is typically what people picture when they think of Rome. In its heyday, the amphitheater sat up to eighty thousand spectators and hosted gladiatorial contests, animal hunts and other—often deadly—public displays. In India, the Taj Mahal is a white marble mausoleum with intricate carvings and dazzling gems. Today, the Taj Mahal, which was made by Mughal emperor Shah Jahan in memory of his beloved wife, Mumtaz Mahal, is a UNESCO World Heritage Site and a symbol of eternal love.

In Arizona, however, none of these sights come close to Grand Canyon's jaw-dropping glory. Carved by the roaring Colorado River over millions of years, this vast chasm stretches for 277 miles and plunges to depths of over 1 mile, easily earning its designation as one of the seven natural wonders of the world. It's no wonder Fred Harvey chose this majestic site for his El Tovar Hotel, a beacon of old world charm and timeless elegance.

Beneath its grand façade, however, lies a haunting tale: the creepy tale of Fred Harvey and the ghostly apparitions that wander the halls of this iconic establishment.

When one thinks of western hospitality in the late 1800s, many think of entrepreneur Fred Harvey and his famed Harvey houses, which were known for employing young woman hosts known as Harvey Girls. Born in England in 1835, Harvey immigrated to the United States in 1853 and soon found success in the restaurant business, which grew proportionately in 1876. Harvey then partnered with the Atchison, Topeka and Santa Fe Railway to create a chain of high-quality restaurants and hotels along the rail lines.

Called Harvey Houses, these restaurants and hotels set new standards for service and cuisine in what was then frontier land. But Harvey's crowning achievement, most concur, is that magnificent structure still located at the Grand Canyon.

The El Tovar sits within walking distance of the edge of Arizona's own natural wonder. The grand hotel has welcomed guests since it opened in 1905. The hotel was designed in the chalet style by architect Charles Whittlesey, and its construction was a grand undertaking. Building materials were transported to what was then a remote location along the Rim, creating an architectural marvel for visitors to northern Arizona. The chalet style, according to the *Cambridge Dictionary*, refers to a wooden house typically found in mountainous areas or a structure built in that style that is used by people while on holiday.

Behind the opulence of the El Tovar resides something a bit darker, however. Both guests and staff have reported experiencing eerie occurrences and unexplained phenomena at the El Tovar over the years—some quite chilling. There have even been reports of shadowy figures seen wandering the halls of the hotel, usually well past the time when most would be comfortable in their bed. Since the early twentieth century, rumors and stories of haunted experiences have been shared among residents of the Grand Canyon and those who worked at the hotel. The first sightings, odd sounds and voices heard when no one else seemed to be around date to the early 1900s, shortly after the hotel first opened its doors.

It's said a ghost that once welcomed a couple to a holiday party at the El Tovar was none other than Fred Harvey himself. The gentleman was described as being polite and very well dressed. The chills came later when the man seemed to vanish without a trace.

Another popular ghost story from around the El Tovar is that of Pirl, whose grave can be found in the El Tovar parking lot. Historians speculate about whether Pirl is the spirit of a dead Harvey Girl or cowboy. While no one knows the answer, there have been a handful of reports over the years of a figure in black seen standing at the grave, but it usually disappears behind the nearby Hopi House.

The website Haunted Places is filled with ghostly tales from the Grand Canyon, and there, rattled visitors to the El Tovar have shared their own ghostly experiences of sleeping within the hotel's walls. This includes stories of being awoken in the evenings to the sight of an old man standing over them in bed. The man, described as being in his seventies with wispy gray hair and dressed in a long-sleeved flannel, is said to stand quietly by the

An assortment of shadowy figures, some long since passed, have been observed wandering the dark halls of Grand Canyon's El Tovar Hotel since it opened in 1905. *Illustration by Jason McLean.*

side of the bed. Other incidents have described the old man wearing a suit from the 1900s. Other stories describe lamps turning off and on by themselves in the rooms.

Of all the rooms in the El Tovar, none is said to be more haunted than room 33. Guests who have stayed in this room have reported feeling a sense of dread within its walls. Some claims describe disembodied whispers and even laughter heard in the darkness. Others reported that their belongings were rearranged or moved while they slept.

Elite celebrities are among those who reported strange goings-on at the hotel. Theodore Roosevelt, the twenty-sixth president of the United States, stayed at the hotel during one of his visits to the Grand Canyon. It's said he was awoken in the dead of night by the sound of ghostly footsteps echoing through the corridors. Albert Einstein, the renowned physicist, also claimed he experienced paranormal phenomena during his stay there. Einstein, who visited the Grand Canyon in 1931, is reported to have seen strange lights and heard unexplained noises coming from the hotel's empty rooms during his stay.

A haunted location like the El Tovar and others is defined as a dwelling that is said to be inhabited by spirits or entities from beyond the grave. Spirits are said to be the unsettled souls of the deceased that are trapped between the worlds of the living and the dead. Ghosts, on the other hand, are believed to be the manifestations of these spirits, appearing as apparitions or spectral presences that can be seen, heard or felt by the living. While the true nature of ghosts remains a mystery, their presence is often associated with feelings of fear, unease or foreboding.

And while the El Tovar is thought to be one of the Grand Canyon's most haunted sites, it's not the first haunted hotel in the state of Arizona. The state's first recorded haunted house dates to the late nineteenth century in the historic town of Jerome (between Cottonwood and Prescott), which can be found on Cleopatra Hill in the Verde Valley. Jerome, once a booming copper mining town, is considered a hotbed of paranormal activity.

The haunted house in question is Jerome's Connor Hotel, a prominent landmark that was originally built in 1898 by David Connor. Over the years, the Connor Hotel served as a gathering place for miners, businesspeople and travelers. There are numerous stories of paranormal activity at the Connor Hotel, including reports of disembodied footsteps echoing in empty hallways, doors mysteriously opening and closing on their own and sightings of gloomy figures disappearing in the shadows.

One of the Connor Hotel's most famous ghost stories centers on a woman in red. The ghost of a deceased miner is also said to haunt the halls there. Other visitors once claimed their dog was frightened of something on the wall that couldn't be seen. Others claimed the ghost of a long-passed canine can be heard growling in one of the hotel's rooms; it's thought to be a spirit because there is no dog found after investigating the strange clamor. A commentor on the Haunted Places website even claimed she was possessed during her stay there. But whether she was possessed after a visit to the Spirit Room a short walk away or something more demonic remains to be seen.

7

FLAGSTAFF

Hotel Monte Vista and Other Haunts

Two hours by car from the El Tovar is the Flagstaff community, known as a highlight for visitors to northern Arizona. The town is home to more than seventy-six thousand residents, according to the 2020 United States census.

Nestled beneath the shadow of northern Arizona's San Francisco Peaks, Flagstaff has evolved from a railroad town to become a vibrant city known for its culture, education and exhilarating outdoor activities. It offers a fairer climate than the state's more populous communities of Phoenix and Tucson, where summer temperatures climb above one hundred degrees for months at a time. Flagstaff is known as the cooler community.

In 1876, pioneer Thomas F. McMillan established the village along the busy Atlantic and Pacific Railroad. Named for a ponderosa pine flagpole that was used to mark the burgeoning city, Flagstaff soon grew into a robust locality, thanks to its stake along the railroad line. Born in the mid-nineteenth century, McMillan originally hailed from the eastern United States but had his sights set on the American West at an early age. He made his way to the Arizona Territory and, in 1876, arrived in the wilds of northern Arizona. Legend has it that McMillan was the one who named the fledgling settlement Flagstaff. As one of the area's earliest settlers, McMillan played an influential role in its development and assisted in the town's infrastructure needs, such as the construction of roads, bridges and waterways.

Flagstaff is popular for its four seasons: warm summers without Phoenix-level heat, crisp autumns, cold winters and colorful springs. At an elevation of over seven thousand feet, Flagstaff is also known for being a training ground for athletes of all sorts.

Throughout its history, Flagstaff has been home to an army of notable individuals, including John W. Weatherford, a pioneer and entrepreneur and the person Weatherford Street is named after. Weatherford was born in 1840 in Missouri and made his way to Arizona in the late 1860s. By 1876, he had moved to Flagstaff and opened a mercantile store that catered to the needs of the town's residents and travelers. Weatherford found himself interested in local politics and went on to be elected mayor.

Since Weatherford's death in 1934, his ghost is believed to haunt various locations throughout the city, particularly the Weatherford Hotel, which bears his name. Built in 1900 by Weatherford himself, the hotel is thought to be one of the city's most haunted sites, with ghostly appearances made by not just Weatherford himself but also others. Reports of haunted encounters at the Weatherford Hotel are plentiful and include unexplained footsteps, mysterious knocks and shadowy figures lurking in the corridors well past sunset. These days, the Weatherford is most well known for being the site of the city's popular New Year's Eve celebration, the Pinecone Drop.

There are hundreds of historic locations in Flagstaff said to be occupied by those long dead. One of Flagstaff's most iconic landmarks is the historic Hotel Monte Vista, which opened on New Year's Day 1927. Monte Vista, which means "mountain view" in Spanish, is known locally as the Monte V and was named by a twelve-year-old who won a naming contest. The hotel became a popular destination for travelers and celebrities who were passing through the area. Famous guests, including John Wayne, Bing Crosby and Clark Gable, have stayed there over the years. Zane Grey, the popular western author, also loved the hotel and frequently featured it in his writing.

Besides its historic status, the Monte V is also known as one of the most haunted hotels in the state. Frightened visitors have reported their own personal encounters over the years through shared stories and online chatter.

Designed by prominent architect Charles E. Whittlesey, the Monte V features stucco walls, terra-cotta accents and ornate wrought-iron details. With seventy-three guest rooms, a lavish lobby and a stylish rooftop bar, the hotel quickly became a favorite among tourists, celebrities and locals alike. During the Prohibition era, the hotel's underground cocktail lounge, known as the Monte Vista Cocktail Lounge, became a notorious hot spot for bootleggers. Ask any local, and you might hear stories of a network of secret tunnels beneath the hotel, which allowed smugglers to discreetly transport illegal liquor.

Over the years, hotel guests and staff members alike have reported eerie encounters and unexplained phenomena, ranging from spectral apparitions to chilling cold spots. One well-known tale is that of the phantom bellboy, thought to be behind a variety of pranks, such as moving belongings, blinking lights and making ghostly phone calls and unnatural sounds. A handful of reports indicate the spirit is particularly fond of room 410 and say it has been known to knock on the door unannounced.

Room 305 is believed to be the most haunted of the hotel's many haunted rooms. Reports of a woman reclining in a rocking chair near the window are legion. A few occupants, guests and hotel staff have claimed they've seen the rocking chair moving on its own. Knocking sounds emanate from the closet as well. The consensus is that the room is inhabited by the ghost of an old woman who used to be a lodger there and would frequently spend her afternoons rocking in the chair.

One popular story concerns room 306, where guests allege eerie encounters happen regularly, particularly with the men who stay in that room. The story of that room is about a party of three, one man and the two women of the night he brought to his room. The two ladies would not survive to see the sunrise. It's said the man, after murdering the women, tossed their bodies from the window to the street below. The two women, having died a gruesome death, are believed by many to haunt the room to this day. It's believed they hold a grudge against men who stay in the room. And according to the stories shared by locals and hotel staff, men have reported having strange dreams while sleeping the room—dreams of being strangled. Others have shared they had a feeling of being watched while alone in the room.

Another widely told ghostly tale from the Hotel Monte Vista is the story of the meat man, a spectral character said to haunt room 220. The man, a long-term hotel lodger, was known for his odd habit of hanging meat from the chandelier in his room. He was found dead in the room by a hotel housekeeper. He'd been dead in the room for three days before his body was found. Guests in the room have reported unusual occurrences, including hearing disembodied voices, coughing, laughter and other noises. There have even been reports of cold hands touching people while they slept. According to a U.S. Ghost Adventures story, a maintenance person was once in the room conducting repairs and turned off all electricity to the room, only to find the television on at full blast when he returned. Not only that, but the blankets had been pulled from the bed and tossed to the floor.

Bank robbers stopped at the bar of the Hotel Monte Vista in 1970 to have a drink. One of them, who'd been shot during the robbery, never walked out of the bar alive. *Illustration by Jason McLean.*

The basement of the Monte V is another hot spot for spectral activity. According to reports, a crying baby has been heard in the basement—but no baby has ever been found abandoned down there. Eyewitnesses alleged they have heard a crying woman there as well, leading believers to conclude the mother (perhaps a lady of the night) was forced to abandon her newborn in the tunnels beneath the hotel. The area near the basement is the site of another legend, that of the shadow man. He's described as a dark, menacing character that brings with him a sense of terror whenever he's around. His identity has never been established.

Other ghostly tales include the sightings of a dancing couple, often seen dancing the night away in the cocktail lounge. What makes this an otherworldly encounter is that the couple is transparent. There's also the story of the bank robbers who celebrated in 1970 by stopping by to have a drink in the Monte V bar, despite one of them having suffered a gunshot wound during the robbery. While celebrating, the man who'd been shot succumbed to his wounds and died right there at the bar. A disembodied voice can sometimes be heard proclaiming "Good morning!" to patrons. Barstools are also said to move about on their own in the bar.

8

PHOENIX

Chills at the Orpheum Theatre

From sleeping arrangements to entertainment, Arizona's haunted locales run the gamut.

Phoenix, Arizona, the state's capital city, is no exception. The city offers a rich history that dates to ancient times. The area was originally inhabited by Natives, including the Hohokam and Pueblo tribes, who developed sophisticated irrigation systems to support their agricultural work in the arid, scorching desert landscape.

Phoenix, as we know it, was founded in 1867, when Jack Swilling, a Confederate soldier, saw the potential for agriculture in the area and started a small farming community near the Salt and Gila Rivers. His community would grow to become Phoenix. Former soldier John Moore later purchased the land and, in 1870, established the first official settlement there, named Phoenix after the famed legendary bird that is believed to die and come alive again, rising from its own ashes. The name symbolized the town's ability to rise from the ruins of its ancient predecessors and flourish in the harsh desert environment.

Phoenix grew quickly, thanks, in part, to the construction of the Maricopa and Phoenix Railroad in 1887. This connected Phoenix to the Southern Pacific Railroad, which allowed for greater development and attracted settlers from around the country. Phoenix quickly became a hub for agriculture and commerce. The Southern Pacific Railroad extended its line into Phoenix, linking the city to major markets and opening new opportunities for economic growth. Newspaper reports from the period heralded the arrival of the railroad as nothing more than a transformative event.

Phoenix was incorporated in 1881 and became the capital of the Arizona Territory in 1889, and in 1912, it became the state capital when Arizona achieved statehood. Throughout the early twentieth century, Phoenix continued to expand, thanks to an increase in agriculture, mining and the onset of World War II, which brought new military bases to the area. Then came the invention of cool air in the desert. Air conditioning was the driving force for the subsequent population boom. When desert living became more bearable, thanks to AC, people flocked to the Southwest to start a new life in the sunshine.

As of 2024, Phoenix is the fifth-largest city in the United States by population, with over 1,608,139 residents within its city limits and over 4.7 million in the metropolitan area. Phoenix has been home to historical icons as well. Dwight B. Heard, a businessperson and philanthropist, played a significant role in the development of Phoenix's agricultural industry. Heard was also the original owner of the *Arizona Republican* newspaper, known today as the *Arizona Republic*.

In Arizona—and Phoenix in particular—the name Barry Goldwater is a recognizable one. Goldwater was a five-term U.S. senator and the Republican Party's presidential nominee for the 1964 presidential election. Born in Phoenix in 1909, Goldwater played a key role in the expansion of Phoenix's economy, especially when it comes to aviation and retail markets. He helped establish the Phoenix-based Scenic Airlines and went on to serve as the president of Goldwater's, a downtown Phoenix department store that was owned by his family.

When it comes to politics, Goldwater represented Arizona in the United States Senate from 1953 to 1965 and from 1969 to 1987. His political philosophy, called Goldwater conservatism, emphasized limited government, individual liberty and a strong national defense. Goldwater's presidential campaign in 1964 reshaped the political landscape of the United States, though he lost his presidential bid to Lyndon B. Johnson. It's commonly believed that Goldwater's candidacy energized grassroots activists and paved the way for President Ronald Reagan and the current conservative movement.

In his hometown, Goldwater championed initiatives to preserve the natural beauty of Arizona, including the establishment of the Central Arizona Project, a massive water diversion plan that transformed the region's agricultural landscape. Many landmarks in Phoenix bear Goldwater's name, including the Barry M. Goldwater Terminal at Phoenix Sky Harbor International Airport and Barry Goldwater High School in the northern part of the city.

Thanks to the contributions of people like Moore and Goldwater, Phoenix is now home to museums, art galleries and performing arts venues, including the Heard Museum, which highlights Native art and culture, and the Phoenix Art Museum, which features a collection of new and classic works. Phoenix's natural attractions include Camelback Mountain, Papago Park and South Mountain Park.

The Orpheum Theater in downtown Phoenix is a historic landmark that has been an integral part of the city's cultural scene for over ninety years. Constructed in 1929, the theater has, throughout its history, hosted vaudeville shows, Broadway productions and even concerts. Besides its rich additions to Phoenix's culture, the theater has a dark side as well.

Vaudeville was once a popular form of entertainment, and cities across the country erected theaters to accommodate the demand for live performances, Phoenix included. A group of area businesspeople sought to cash in on the trend when they constructed the Orpheum, designed by the architectural firm of Lescher and Mahoney. The construction of the Orpheum Theater began in 1928 and was completed the following year at an estimated cost of $750,000, a generous sum back then. The theater was designed in the Spanish Baroque Revival style, with ornate detailing, arched windows and decorative terra-cotta embellishments.

The beautiful interior is often said to be a highlight of the Orpheum Theater, which includes a massive lobby adorned with marble columns, a gilded ceiling and a majestic staircase that leads to the balcony level. The theater itself features plush seating, intricate plasterwork and a domed ceiling with a stunning mural depicting scenes from Greek mythology.

The Orpheum opened to the public on January 5, 1929, with a performance by the vaudeville troupe Ted Lewis and His Orchestra. Over the years, the theater became a popular venue for a variety of live entertainment acts, including plays, musicals, dance performances and concerts.

In addition to hosting live performances, the Orpheum Theater has served as a palatial movie theater, screening classic Hollywood films. The theater's state-of-the-art projection equipment and luxurious surroundings made it a favorite destination for moviegoers in Phoenix.

The theater has undergone several renovations and restorations over the years, and in 1985, it was added to the National Register of Historic Places in recognition of its architectural significance and cultural importance to the Phoenix community. Today, the Orpheum Theater continues to be a vibrant cultural hub in downtown Phoenix, hosting a diverse array of performances and events. Along with Broadway musicals and touring productions to local theater companies and community concerts, the theater also hosts educational programs, workshops and outreach programs.

It's also home to a different kind of spectacle, that of the more spectral variety, including the ghostly presence simply known as Maddie. Visitors and staff alike have reported sightings of a ghostly figure of a young girl, though she's commonly believed to primarily inhabit the balcony. Officially, there are no records that indicate a girl by that name or any of its variations has had any connection to the theater, according to Phoenix Ghosts. Reports have typically placed her near the stage or in the dressing rooms. A 12 News report in 2019 indicated that Maddie is also known to tap people on the shoulder and even to shush patrons who may be getting a little too chatty during a show. She's even thought to have once slapped a man in the back of the head. The man, according to the stories, was more interested in making out with his girlfriend than what was happening on the stage. She's also remembered for once stopping a production in its tracks, albeit briefly. Dancers in a Chinese production once stopped dancing during a performance after a group of them observed the little girl watching from the balcony and then walking off the balcony before disappearing into thin air. They quickly continued with the show, despite their shock.

Maddie isn't the only ghost thought to haunt the Orpheum, however.

More recently, in 2019, visitors to the theater encountered another ghost: a woman dressed in a period dress with netting over her head. An employee observed and had words with the woman. According to Phoenix Ghosts, which offers tours of the theater, he believed he was speaking to a real person. But he realized later that she wasn't among the living. The Orpheum Theater is believed to be home to at least four ghosts, one of which may be the spirit of Harry Nance, one of the theater's original owners.

The theater is so well known for its haunted happenings that paranormal investigators contact the theater regularly to stay overnight in the hopes of recording the supernatural. The theater's ghost tours, held during the Halloween season, often sell out.

This brings us to another Arizona theater with the same name. Flagstaff's Orpheum Theater was constructed in 1911 by local businessperson John Weatherford, who we met in a prior chapter. The theater, which opened in late October that year, offered viewers the opportunity to catch the latest craze: movies. In its early years, the theater changed locations, was smothered in a heavy snowstorm and even underwent some name changes, from the Majestic Theatre to the Empress Theater. In 1916, Weatherford finally settled on Orpheum, in honor of the Greek god, according to the book *Historic Tales of Flagstaff*, by Kevin Schindler and Michael Kitt.

The theater's northern Arizona location, at 15 West Aspen Avenue, is also said to house a handful of unhappy spirits. Reports of creepy sounds, shadowy figures and shivering sensations have been documented there. Spirits at the venue seem to congregate in two locations there, the upper balcony and in the men's bathroom. There is also an urban legend surrounding a man who allegedly hanged himself from the roof there. The latter story may just be a legend, but the stories of the man, who remains unknown, persist to this day.

On the upper balcony, an evening janitor once reported seeing a dark figure gliding down the aisles in the dead of night. Thinking someone had entered the theater, the janitor went to investigate, only to find the figure had vanished and he was alone. Another ghostly entity at the Flagstaff Orpheum Theater is that of an older woman wearing all white. She's never seen for long, but when she is, she's viewed by a railing.

When it comes to the men's bathroom, no one is quite sure why it's haunted, but believers claim it is very haunted, nonetheless. Disembodied footsteps are often heard there. Others have even reported having the sensation of mild electric shocks when walking into the bathroom. Another account of paranormal activity, allegedly witnessed by former employees, said that all the bathroom sinks once turned on by themselves. And not only that—all the toilets flushed as well.

Back in Phoenix, haunted locations seem as common as saguaro cactus. From Phoenix's haunted theater and various hotels all the way to haunted cemeteries, the Valley of the Sun is home to a plethora of paranormal phenomena. Of the smattering of haunted locations there, paranormal fans believe the most haunted site, aside from the Orpheum Theater, is the Hotel San Carlos, also known as the San Carlos Hotel, found at 202 North Central Avenue. After opening in 1928, the hotel was publicized as the first high rise with air conditioning. This historic hotel has long been rumored to be haunted by not just one but a handful of spirits. The building itself was listed in the National Register of Historic Places in 1983.

One of the most well-known stories about the hotel involves the ghost of Los Angeles resident Leone Jensen, a young blond woman who tragically fell to her death from the roof of the hotel in the early morning hours of a day in May 1928 while visiting Phoenix. According to newspaper accounts from the time, it was ruled Jensen died by suicide, but some believe foul play was involved. Guests and hotel employees over the years have reported feeling cold spots in the building, hearing the sounds of footsteps when no one seems to be around and even encountering ghostly apparitions in the halls.

Jensen's plummet was notable for the notes she left behind before ascending to the hotel's seventh-floor roof. She left them on her person; some were addressed to friends while another was addressed to the hotel management, and one gave funeral instructions. Her body was found on Monroe Street by a passing police officer. Just over one month after opening, the hotel marked its first death. Jensen had been in room 720 for two days, according to a 2019 story in AZ Central.

"Bury me in my tan dress and tan high-heeled slippers," her note read to the undertaker.

An apparition that is seen in the halls and sometimes standing quietly at the foot of someone's hotel bed has been attributed to Jensen. The ghost has been described as a forlorn woman in white. Jensen's body, according to reports, was found dressed in a rose-colored dress with a tan coat and light shoes with stockings. Tales of her demise vary, as some claim she stepped off the roof that fateful morning after battling personal health problems. Others claim she came to Phoenix to see a boyfriend, possibly a bell boy who worked at a nearby hotel, and that he may have had something to do with her death. In any event, some claim they have seen her, even years after her death, on the roof of the hotel.

Besides the spirit of Jensen, other hauntings occur at the hotel, including the sound of giggling ghostly children, usually around the basement where a well was once located.

Another haunted hot spot in Phoenix is the Rosson House Museum, located in Heritage Square at 113 North Sixth Street. Built in 1895, this Queen Anne, Victorian–era mansion is said to be haunted by the spirit of a caretaker who was shot dead right outside the house in the 1980s. His spirit has been said to occasionally appear in the Victorian home, fully formed, to both visitors and guests. It's rumored that most of his appearances occur near the stairs. Dark shadows have been seen at the museum, and doors have been known to lock and unlock without being touched. The unused fireplace has also been known to give off a supernatural heat.

Phoenix's Pioneer and Military Memorial Park, a historic cemetery founded in 1884, is located at Fourteenth Avenue and Jefferson Street and is made up of seven cemeteries. Over the years, numerous reports of paranormal activity have been documented at the cemetery, including sightings of shadowy figures and strange orbs of light. According to newspaper accounts, visitors have reported feeling an overwhelming sense of unease while exploring the grounds. Ghost hunters flock to the cemetery in the hopes of recording the spirits. One famous occupant of the cemetery is the notorious lost Dutchman Jacob Waltz. Born around 1810, Waltz is famous for his alleged discovery of a gold deposit somewhere in the Superstition Mountains, which overlook the Phoenix metropolitan area. Countless treasure hunters have searched for the Lost Dutchman Mine over the years, but none have ever been successful. Historians believe that the spirits of those who died searching for the treasure still haunt the mountains, guarding their secret from would-be fortune-seekers.

9

TUCSON

Hotel Congress Scares

Just south of Phoenix and situated in the Sonoran Desert, we find the city of Tucson, known as one of the oldest continuously inhabited cities in the United States. The area was first occupied by Native peoples, including the Hohokam, who created an extensive network of irrigation canals in the region.

When the Spanish arrived in the sixteenth century, this marked a significant turning point in the history of the area. They established the Presidio San Agustín del Tucsón in 1692, which then constituted a military fort that served as a strategic colonization outpost and served to help shelter the settlers from attack.

During the eighteenth and nineteenth centuries, Tucson became known as a growing frontier town and an important stopping point along the El Camino Real, or "the royal road," which connected the Spanish colonies of Mexico with other settlements in what is now known as California. The area served as a hub for trade and commerce, and merchants, traders and settlers congregated in the region.

The Gadsden Purchase, a treaty between the United States and Mexico signed in 1854, transferred Tucson and the rest of southern Arizona to the United States. The city's population grew rapidly following the acquisition, as Americans moved westward in search of land and opportunity. Tucson became the capital of the Arizona Territory in 1867, solidifying the city's status as a regional center of government and commerce.

One of Tucson's most significant historical events occurred in 1880, when the Southern Pacific Railroad reached the city and connected it to the rest of the country. Thanks to that set of train tracks, Tucson enjoyed greater commerce opportunities. The community became more accessible to new residents and entrepreneurs, not to mention that investors were quick to move to the area. Businesses, such as mining and agriculture, expanded in southern Arizona as a result. Copper, silver, agriculture and more were made accessible thanks to the rail line. As a result, storage warehouses were needed, leading to a boom in infrastructure in the region. Aside from transporting goods, the railroad is also credited with changing the cultural landscape of the community, as the city became a hub for everyone from every culture and ethnicity who was interested in moving to the rough-around-the-edges frontier town. Immigrants from Mexico, Europe and Asia all made the community home. In 1880, Tucson's population was estimated at just above forty thousand.

Tucson's downtown continued to grow, and in 1918, the Hotel Congress and the Rialto Theater were built. Tucson became a center for military activity during World War II as well with the establishment of Davis-Monthan Air Force Base and other nearby military installations. Today, visitors come to Tucson for a variety of reasons, including to experience what Tucsonans call the big small-town vibe. Tourists come to see the Arizona-Sonora Desert Museum, which explores the region's natural history and biodiversity, and experience the Mission San Xavier del Bac, a historic Spanish mission founded in 1692. Some come to stay at one of the resorts located throughout the city and surrounding areas. Annual events, such as the Tucson Gem and Mineral Show and the Tucson Festival of Books, draw thousands of visitors to the city each year.

Tucson's draw comes not just from rocks and books, however, but also from more spiritual attractions. And the Hotel Congress is one such locale. The historic hotel is one of Tucson's most haunted locations and a popular stop for ghost hunters.

The Congress officially opened its doors to guests in 1919. Designed by architect William Curlett, the hotel acquired its name from a contest held in 1918 by the *Arizona Daily Star*. Since it was conveniently located near the Southern Pacific Railroad depot, the hotel was a luxurious yet sensible choice for travelers. In 1934, legendary gangster John Dillinger and his posse hid out at the Hotel Congress while on the run from law enforcement. Unfortunately for them—but lucky for the law—a fire broke out, subsequently leading to their capture. The arrest of Dillinger made national news at the time and made the Hotel Congress a popular destination for years. Dillinger and his

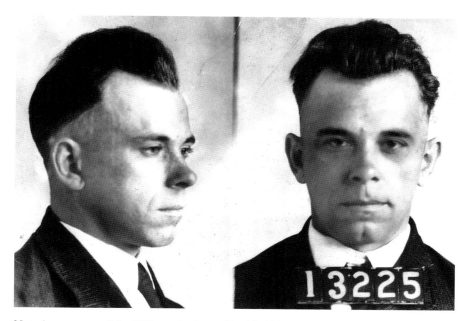

Notorious gangster John Dillinger is pictured in this 1924 mug shot, taken for the Indiana State Penitentiary. Dillinger and his gang made their way to Tucson in 1934. *Indiana State Penitentiary photographic records.*

arrest are honored each January in Tucson, especially at the Hotel Congress, with Dillinger Days.

Today, the Hotel Congress still offers accommodations for its guests and regularly holds live events and dining for locals. Attractions at the hotel include its famous bar and restaurant. While they are not on the menu, the hotel's ghostly residents may also be a draw for countless paranormal investigators.

Two rooms are said to be quite haunted: 214 and 242. The spirits said to inhabit those rooms are both rumored to have died by suicide. Room 214 is said to be inhabited by a strange character known as "the Victorian gentleman," while room 242 is said to be haunted by a female spirit known simply as "the woman in the white dress." Rooms 212 and 220 are also said to be paranormal hot spots. Room 212 is known as the haunt of the "locksmith apprentice," while 220 is inhabited by none other than the "tricky veteran." All four of these rooms are available to those seeking a little adventure in their hotel stay.

While there are variations to the stories, room 242 has often been called the "Suicide Room," due to the fact that the woman in white is thought to have taken her own life there. The incident is alleged to have occurred in the 1940s, according to a 2013 article in the *Tucson Weekly*. The unhappy woman was engaged in a standoff with police from her room when she shot herself. The deadly bullet, it's said, smashed through a bathroom wall and into the closet. The hole can still be viewed there. The spirit has allegedly sat on the bed, stared at visitors and even attempted to touch them. The spirit is also believed to have whispered in the ear of a paranormal investigator or two.

In room 214, meanwhile, it is said a depressed man shot himself with a shotgun he'd rigged for his own death and is now eternally stuck in the room. He's been seen at the window dressed in what witnesses have described as a seersucker suit. According to stories, the man has unplugged the vacuum from the wall when room service has been inside. In order to continue vacuuming the place, according to the stories, the cleaners must play 1920s-era music, which calms the restless spirit. Other accounts have described the appearance of a bloody handprint on the wall.

A World War II veteran believed to have been a longtime guest of the hotel haunts a number of locations within the building, though he is thought to most often haunt the bar on the first floor, where he used to hang out. Sightings indicate he's seen at one end of the bar. According to the stories, this veteran is a harmless spiritual barfly—unless he doesn't enjoy the music on the jukebox. He's known to turn up music he likes and lower the volume on songs he doesn't like.

Vince is the name given to another spirit thought to dwell within the Congress. He's often seen enjoying the scenery while looking out of a window on the second floor. He's also thought to have been fond of borrowing butter knives from the Cup Café, found within the hotel, while he was among the living. Now, hotel staff continue to find butter knives in random spots throughout the second floor.

Other spirits said to roam the halls of the Hotel Congress include the spirits of two children, commonly believed to be the ghosts of a little boy and a little girl, both around seven years old. The children died either from a disease or as the result of an accident, depending on which version of the story one hears. Guests have also reported the apparition of a man in period clothing. It's believed he's one of the scores of travelers who passed through the hotel over the years. Others have alleged they encountered shadowy figures moving about the rooms and disappearing into thin air. A man was also shot dead during a card game that was held on the first floor of the hotel in the 1920s or 1930s. He's been seen wearing a pin-striped suit. Accusations of cheating are believed to have been what led to the murder, according to the Haunted Houses website.

Over the years, paranormal investigators have flocked to the Hotel Congress. Investigators there have used electromagnetic field (EMF) meters, infrared cameras, voice recorders and more in the hopes of finding definitive proof of the afterlife within the hotel's halls and rooms. Zak Bagans, the host of the popular television series *Ghost Adventures*, visited the hotel with his team and conducted his own investigation there over the course of several nights. Jason Hawes, a cofounder of The Atlantic Paranormal Society (TAPS) and one of the stars of the TV show *Ghost Hunters*, also visited the hotel and performed his own investigation. Other paranormal researchers and investigators who have made their way to the Hotel Congress include members of the Paranormal Research Society (PRS), the Ghost Research Society (GRS) and psychic mediums.

Certain believers think the hotel is indeed haunted by restless spirits from its past, while others remain skeptical, claiming natural causes or psychological factors have led to the belief that the hotel is haunted.

Haunted stories of the hotel have been featured in local media as well. Several newspapers and TV news channels have documented the eerie encounters and ghostly sightings alleged to have occurred there. Local journalists have interviewed guests and staff members who have experienced the paranormal phenomena firsthand. The hotel has been featured in the *Arizona Daily Star*, KGUN 9 and elsewhere over the years.

Of course, the Hotel Congress isn't alone in its distinction of being one of the city's spooky haunts. The city's other haunted locations include the Fox Theater, the Pioneer Hotel, the Rialto Theater and the Santa Rita Hotel, and there have even been reports of phantasmagorical phenomena on the campus of the University of Arizona.

The Fox Theater, which opened in 1930 and closed in 1974, is located at 17 West Congress Street in downtown Tucson. The theater was eventually reopened in 2006 and is now rumored to be haunted by a few restless spirits. These spirits include the famed "begging man." While not much is known about the begging man's identity, he has been witnessed begging for spare change in the lobby. When people have attempted to give him money, the change simply falls through his hands to the floor, and the man himself disappears.

The spirit of a little girl has also been observed giggling in the lower lobby of the theater, according to an article from the website This Is Tucson. Props have also been known to move on their own during live performances there.

The Pioneer Hotel can still be found downtown at 100 North Stone Street, but it is now an office building. It was also the site of a tragic fire in 1970 that claimed the lives of twenty-nine people. Many believe the spirits of those who perished in the fire still haunt the building. Visitors and employees have reported hearing ghostly screams and seeing apparitions in the hallways. It's rumored that ghostly occurrences are primarily observed on the hotel's roof and that there are dark forces—entities, witnesses say—that congregate in the basement.

The Rialto Theater, another historic venue in downtown Tucson, located at 318 East Congress Street, opened in 1920 and is said to be haunted by the spirit of a projectionist. Other reports of haunted occurrences there include cold spots and the appearance of a mysterious woman who then suddenly disappears. Two people are alleged to have died at the theater: one was a 1940s piano player who was crushed by his own piano in the orchestra pit, and the other was a man who died during a screening at the theater. One, or both, are said to haunt the regal theater.

The Santa Rita Hotel, which no longer stands at the corner of East Broadway Boulevard and South Sixth Avenue, was a popular spot for visitors when it first opened in February 1904. Over its years of operation, many notables spent time there, including Martin Luther King Jr., who stayed there in 1962. The hotel, thought to be haunted, was demolished in 2009, as it had sat abandoned since 2005. Lights on the fourth floor would flicker on and off, footsteps were heard on the stairs and full-bellied laughter had been noted coming from the building when no one was thought to be inside.

The University of Arizona's campus is home to several haunted locations, including the modern languages building and the Alexander Berger Memorial Fountain at Old Main. Rumors and tales spread around campus state that a young woman was murdered and deposited in a well on the site of the modern languages building, where she still wanders and is seen with flowing black hair and dressed in a shawl. The spirit of Alexander Berger, a well-known Tucson philanthropist in the early 1900s, has made appearances on campus as well. He's been seen, according to campus stories, in the mist created by the fountain on cold mornings.

Let's turn now from higher education to six-shooters and outlaws.

10

TOMBSTONE

Bullets at the Bird Cage Theatre

Fans of the Wild West, whether on screen, in books or via a love of history, will recognize the name Tombstone, especially those familiar with the story of the O.K. Corral gunfight.

Founded in 1879, Tombstone is located a little over an hour's drive from downtown Tucson and is often visited by history buffs and Arizona residents alike.

Prospector Ed Schieffelin, who was staying in what was then Camp Huachuca, inadvertently became Tombstone's father. He struck out on his own, despite warnings that he might encounter Apache along the way, and according to the stories, he was told the only thing he'd find prospecting would be his own tombstone. Gruesome predictions aside, Schieffelin unearthed a silver mine of his own and named it Tombstone as a nod to the naysayers. By 1879, new residents were beginning to ride in; this included shooters, homesteaders, women of the night and other prospectors. By 1881, Tombstone had a population between four and five thousand and quickly became one of the wealthiest mining towns in the Southwest. By the late 1890s, the town's population had peaked at about fifteen thousand.

Little would be remembered about Tombstone, however, were it not for the deadly gunfight that broke out on October 26, 1881. The notorious gunfight at the O.K. Corral lasted just a handful of seconds but went down in history. It earned Tombstone the nickname "The Town Too Tough to Die."

On that day, Wyatt, Virgil and Morgan Earp, and, of course, the infamous Doc Holliday, exchanged a barrage of bullets with Billy Clanton and his pals, "the Cowboys," Frank and Tom McLaury. The Clanton and McLaury families were employed by a nearby cattle ranch and often moonlighted their services for extra cash. They weren't above much when it came to their side jobs. They'd run across the Earps and Holliday the day before the shootout, just as the outlaws had torn into Tombstone for supplies. The Earps formed the law enforcement side of the battle. With their prior run-in on the minds of everyone there, the two groups duked it out in a vacant lot, just behind the corral at the end of Fremont Street, around 3:00 p.m. A shot was fired, though which side fired that first round is open for debate, and the historic battle began. Virgil Earp, according to accounts, fired a shot into Billy Clanton's chest. Holliday, they say, let off a shotgun blast that hit Tom McLaury in the chest. Over thirty rounds were fired in about thirty seconds. When the dust was settled, the McLaury brothers and Clanton were dead. Their two accomplices, Ike Clanton and Billy Claiborne, took off on foot. Doc Holliday and Virgil and Morgan Earp were wounded as well.

Today, Tombstone is a popular tourist attraction for historians and fans of western lore. The city features the corral, which is still standing,

Approximately thirty rounds were fired in thirty seconds during the notorious gunfight at the O.K. Corral in Tombstone, the "town too tough to die." *Illustration by Jason McLean.*

and reenactments full of cowboys and simulated gunfire; plus, the famed Boothill Cemetery is just down the road, and historic, old-time saloons are open every day.

The gunfight at the O.K. Corral has gone down in history as the Old West personified, immortalized in books, movies and television shows. Today, the site of the gunfight is a popular tourist attraction in Tombstone, drawing visitors from around the world who come to learn about the history and legends of the American West.

According to western paranormal reports, the spirits of those killed in the gunfight may still haunt the streets of Tombstone, particularly around the site of the O.K. Corral. Visitors to the historic landmark have reported seeing shadowy figures moving among the old buildings and have heard gunfire from the great beyond.

Aside from the scene of the famed gunfight at the O.K. Corral, Tombstone is just a short distance from the site of the deadly Bisbee Massacre of 1883, in which five men were killed during a stagecoach robbery. When the silver mines dried up, Tombstone did as well, though its reputation persisted. Tombstone today, with a population of just under 1,500, is known for its sordid history and Wild West shows. Visitors can explore historic sites like the O.K. Corral and the Bird Cage Theatre, take a ride on a stagecoach and even watch reenactments of famous gunfights.

Visitors to Tombstone flock to the iconic Bird Cage Theatre, found at Sixth and Allen Streets, a former saloon and theater that held its own during the tough town's heyday. The Bird Cage Theatre is notorious for its former life as a gambling hall and brothel, but it's also known everywhere for its status as one of the most haunted places in the United States.

Built in 1881 during Tombstone's silver mining boom by Billy and Lottie Hutchinson, the Bird Cage was constructed where the Elite Theater was once located and opened on Christmas Eve that year. The Elite had burned down in a fire earlier that year. The Hutchinsons, recognizing a need for entertainment and cultural enrichment in the bustling community, built the Bird Cage Theatre, the crown jewel of Tombstone. Though it was originally intended for upscale, family-oriented productions, the theater quickly resorted to raunchier forms of entertainment.

It didn't take long before the Bird Cage Theatre became a staple of the lore of the Wild West and an example of the lawlessness of the dusty, hot frontier. The theater, which hosted vaudeville performances and even boxing matches, was known for offering patrons of one nefarious occupation or another the Bird Cage Balcony, a special spot reserved for those who could afford such amenities. Women of the night were also known to occupy that section.

A typical night at the Bird Cage included performances by can-can dancers, gambling, the sort of adventures expected in a red-light district and a brawl or two. The theater even had a basement casino for those who hoped to make a bit of money rather than spend it all. Violence was a common occurrence at the Bird Cage. The gambling and red-light district attracted a tough crew, and fistfights, gunfights and every other kind of fight were common there. The theater had a reputation for being one of the most dangerous and deadly establishments in the Wild West. More than 140 bullet holes can still be seen in its walls to this day. Legend has it that a single poker game ran there continuously for eight years, earning it the title "the longest poker game in history."

It's not surprising, based off the bullet holes alone, that the theater was the site of at least twenty-six deaths due to gunfights, suicides and stabbings. One of the more famous incidents is that of Margarita, a Tombstone madam known as the Painted Lady (also known as the Belle of the Birdcage), who had her heart carved out of her body there. A rival madam, Gold Dollar Gertie, or Little Gertie the Gold Dollar, allegedly murdered Margarita. The stabbing stemmed, historians believe, from a love triangle involving the two women and a man named Billy Milgreen. According to legend, Gertie was never charged with the murder, as no murder weapon was found on her body when she was finally apprehended. The knife she used didn't vanish, however, as it was found years later behind the Bird Cage Theatre. Those interested in seeing the knife may find it on display there.

Over the years, witnesses have claimed they saw the dark-haired Margarita within the walls of the theater. She's typically observed on the stage. One report even claimed she stood naked behind the curtain. Her gravestone, meanwhile, can be found at Tombstone's Boothill Graveyard, marked with the words "Stabbed by Gold Dollar."

Margarita's isn't the only ghost to love the stage at the Bird Cage. Shadowy figures, believed to be the spirits of long-dead stagehands, have also been seen behind the scenes near the stage. Other phantasmagorical occurrences include the thick smell of cigar smoke hanging around inside, despite the fact smoking hasn't been allowed inside the theater for years. Loud yelling and laughter, as if a party were in progress, have also been heard there when the building was empty. The "weeping woman" is another famous presence at the Bird Cage Theatre. Said the be the spirit of a woman named Carmelita Gimenes, the weeping woman is believed

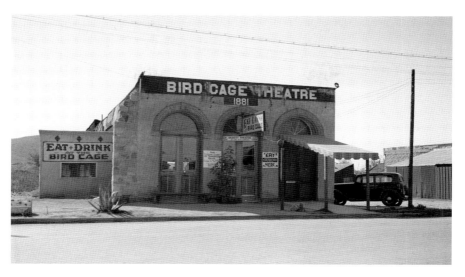

The diminutive Bird Cage Theater, pictured here in 1940, still entertains Tombstone's wild-minded visitors, though many of them may be ghosts. *United States Library of Congress's Prints and Photographs Division.*

by many to have worked as a sex worker at the theater before she killed herself by drinking arsenic around 1888. Her spirit remains in the form of a weeping woman. A statue of Wyatt Earp is also the basis for ghostly happenings. It's said a hat that is placed atop the statue's head is often tossed around as if it is being pulled by invisible strings.

Another spirit said to haunt the Bird Cage is the "lady in white." Dressed in finery not often associated with the rough-and-tumble town, the lady in white has been seen on more than one occasion, though she has never interacted with anyone during her visits. Suzie is another spirit said to haunt the balcony. Suzie was alleged to have been a performer during the theater's heyday, and stories indicate she was madly in love and ultimately betrayed and murdered by her lover. It's said she has haunted the balcony ever since.

The Bird Cage is now a museum and historic landmark where visitors can admire the theater's original look, see artifacts from the Wild West era and, of course, view the building's original bullet-riddled walls. In addition to guided tours and educational programs, the Bird Cage Theatre plays host to extraordinary events, performances and, like elsewhere in the town, Wild West reenactments. The theater even appeared in the 1993 movie *Tombstone*. Its haunted elements have also been featured on various ghost hunting programs, including a 2006 episode of *Ghost Hunters*, 2009 and 2015 episodes of *Ghost Adventures*, a 2009 episode of *Ghost Lab* and others.

Originally founded in 1879, Tombstone has seen its fair share of violence over the years. Victims of that violence may have stuck around as shadows peering from windows. *Illustration by Jason McLean.*

Of course, the Bird Cage isn't the only haunted location in Tombstone. The Crystal Palace Saloon, located at 420 East Allen Street, is one of the town's oldest bars and is said to be populated by the spirits of both miners and cowboys who once caroused there. Visitors have reported hearing glasses clink and raucous laughter echoing in the empty saloon after dark. The sounds of boots and spurs have also been heard there—not to mention reports of a spinning roulette wheel that seems to move on its own. Photographs in the Crystal Palace are known to glow occasionally.

The Tombstone Courthouse, also currently a Tombstone city museum, is said to be haunted by the spirits of both dead inmates and dead law enforcement officers. Visitors have claimed they felt a sense of unease or saw strange orbs of light meandering among the exhibits. Built in 1882, the historic courthouse served as the judicial seat for Cochise County, but today, it's remembered for its cold spots and ghostly visitors, which includes the spirits of long-dead outlaws who were convicted there, saloon girls and even a judge who wanders the halls at night in his black robes.

With Tombstone's rich western history and haunted locales, ghost tours are held there regularly at the locations mentioned in this chapter or any number of the town's other paranormal hot spots.

PART III

UFOs

11

GRAND CANYON

A Four-Thousand-Year-Old Crash

L et's turn from Arizona's haunted attractions to something a bit higher up, though just as chilling. Otherworldly aliens and unidentified objects in the sky can elicit reactions similar to the creeps one experiences when staring face to face with a long-dead gunslinger out of the Old West.

The fascination with unidentifiable objects in the air above us isn't just a modern phenomenon, though the reports of UFOs increased with the advent of humans conquering the skies. Sightings go back much further than the 1940s and the famous crash in Roswell, New Mexico.

Theories about UFOs, or unidentified flying objects, have captivated the human imagination since humankind first glued their eyes to the skies.

But are these extraterrestrial spacecrafts filled with mysterious, green-skinned creatures from another planet or objects with a more down-to-earth explanation? For sky-watchers the answer is simple: the UFOs' shape, often flat and circular; their sheer size in a few cases; their speed; and the fact they make little noise has some convinced that the objects hail from somewhere beyond our atmosphere.

A more earthbound theory holds that these unidentified objects are classified military aircraft made by the world's governments under secrecy—or even that they're the products of other secret projects from business corporations. Aircraft testing happens every day throughout the world, of which the public is not always made aware. Those who hold the view that these craft belong to another planet argue against that point, however, by stating simply that it would be next to impossible to hide the advanced technology needed to pilot these silent, fast-moving objects from the public for long.

Others believe in the theory that these craft hail not from another planet but from our future, and these UFOs aren't spacecraft but time machines. Others believe there are creatures piloting vehicles from outside of our dimension. They may be from Earth, just not our Earth.

Tales of UFOs in Arizona are legion and include notable cases that are still discussed. This includes the Phoenix lights, which are covered in chapter 13, and the abduction of a man near Snowflake, Arizona, which became the basis for the eerie motion picture *Fire in the Sky* and is featured in chapter 14.

Reported sightings have also included tales of alleged crashes and landings in remote areas of northern Arizona, particularly near the Grand Canyon.

American UFO sightings, however, go back a long way. One such observance came from a man named John Winthrop in 1639, who journaled about a "great light in the sky" over Boston, Massachusetts. The sighting was reportedly over Muddy Creek, now located around the famed Fenway Park. Winthrop was the Puritan leader of the Massachusetts Bay Colony and commonly believed to be the first to document a UFO sighting in America. Known as a detailed journal-keeper, detailing the life and struggles in early Massachusetts, Winthrop is also known for his reports of two UFO encounters, one of which suggested that three men in a boat may have been abducted.

He wrote in his journal,

> *In this year one James Everell, a sober, discreet man, and two others, saw a great light in the night at Muddy River. When it stood still, it flamed up, and was about three yards square; when it ran, it was contracted into the figure of a swine: it ran as swift as an arrow towards Charlton* [Charlestown], *and so up and down* [for] *about two or three hours. They were come down in their lighter about a mile, and, when it was over, they found themselves carried quite back against the tide to the place they came from. Divers other credible persons saw the same light, after, about the same place.*

James Savage penned the following footnote about the sighting.

> *This account of an ignis fatuus* [pale light over marshy ground] *may easily be believed on testimony less respectable than that which was adduced. Some operation of the devil, or other power beyond the customary*

agents of nature, was probably imagined by the relaters and hearers of that age, and the wonder of being carried a mile against the tide became important corroboration of the imagination. Perhaps they were wafted [carry lightly], *during the two- or three-hours' astonishment, for so moderate a distance, by the wind; but, if this suggestion be rejected, we might suppose that the eddy* [whirlpool], *flowing always, in our rivers, contrary to the tide in the channel, rather than the meteor, carried their lighter back.*

This sighting was nowhere near the first in the history of the world. The Bible itself is thought to allege the existence of unexplainable aerial phenomena. In the book of Ezekiel, it is said a strange ship appeared from the sky. In Ezekiel 1:4–28, the prophet describes a remarkable vision of a "wheel within a wheel" descending from the sky, accompanied by flashes of lightning and strange creatures with four faces and four wings. UFO theorists suggest that Ezekiel's vision bears striking similarities to modern UFO sightings, with the "wheel within a wheel" often interpreted as a depiction of a spacecraft or flying saucer. Another passage that has sparked speculation is the story of Elijah's ascent to heaven in a "chariot of fire," described in 2 Kings 2:11–12. Interpretations suggest Elijah's chariot may have been a UFO, with the "chariot of fire" representing an otherworldly vehicle capable of transporting him to another existence.

Biblical references to angels and divine messengers from the sky have led some UFO enthusiasts to speculate that aliens indeed visited early civilizations and that those who saw them interpreted them as divine beings.

Historians call these visitors ancient astronauts. Author Erich von Däniken put forth his theory in his book *Chariots of the Gods?.* He argues the case that extraterrestrial encounters may have had a larger influence on human history than many suspect.

These theories, however, remain highly speculative and even controversial among religious scholars and those who apply science toward the understanding of UFOs. Some argue that the "wheel within a wheel" description is merely meant as a symbolic reference to the power of divinity and was never meant to be interpreted as a literal sighting.

Those in Ancient Rome, China and other civilizations contributed their own mysterious tales throughout the centuries. One famous example is the sighting by Roman author Julius Obsequens in his work *Prodigiorum Liber* (*The Book of Prodigies*). In 217 BCE, during the Second Punic War, Obsequens describes a "spectacle of ships" in the sky over Rome, where "a remarkable shape of a ship" was observed floating through the air. Could this have been a fleet of alien craft paying a visit to the Roman Coliseum?

In China, the *Bamboo Annals*, an ancient Chinese text dating to the fourth century BCE, contains references to strange objects in the sky, including flying chariots and glowing orbs. Additionally, Chinese mythology and folklore regularly refer to celestial beings and flying dragons, which could be interpreted as early accounts of UFO encounters. In India, writings have described "vimana," or flying machines piloted by gods and celestial beings. Ancient Sanskrit texts, dating back thousands of years, mention advanced machines capable of traveling through the air and even into orbit.

The Mesopotamian *Epic of Gilgamesh* contains references to celestial objects and encounters with otherworldly beings. In one passage, Gilgamesh describes a "brilliant object" descending from the sky, which ufologists claim describes a potential UFO sighting, though tales from the ancient world and more than a few from the modern era should be taken with a grain of salt.

This brings us to a relic of the ancient world located in Arizona's front yard: the Grand Canyon.

The Grand Canyon, aside from being one of the wonders of the world and a top draw for Arizona tourists, has a history spanning millions of years. Geologists estimate the Grand Canyon was formed over the course of millions of years by the erosive forces of the Colorado River, which carved its way through layers of rock to create the iconic attraction we see now. The oldest exposed rocks there are nearly two billion years old and date to the Precambrian era. For geologists and historians, these rocks provide valuable clues about this planet's early history.

The ancestral Puebloans, known as the Anasazi, lived in the Four Corners region over one thousand years ago. Their presence can still be felt in their dwellings, petroglyphs and other archaeological sites scattered throughout the canyon. The arrival of Europeans in the sixteenth century brought significant changes to the Grand Canyon region. Spanish explorers were among the first Europeans to encounter the canyon, followed by expeditions led by American explorers and surveyors in the nineteenth century.

One of the most famous moments in the history of the Grand Canyon occurred in 1903, when President Theodore Roosevelt visited the canyon and declared it a national monument to preserve its natural beauty for future generations. This proclamation laid the groundwork for the eventual establishment of Grand Canyon National Park in 1919, which remains one of the most visited national parks in the United States.

The elevation of Comanche Point, seen here during a 2013 total cloud inversion, is 7,073 feet. Somewhere below, the remains of a four-thousand-year-old UFO were found. *Grand Canyon National Park.*

This, of course, means the Grand Canyon may have been a draw for visitors for far longer than the Arizona Chamber of Commerce has been around. In fact, some believe visitors from an entirely different world may have made their way to the canyon for reasons known only to them. But their trip to this part of the world ended in a crash approximately four thousand years ago. The UFO, which is estimated to be 102 feet long and 50 feet wide, crashed near Comanche Point. It was discovered, according to sources, lodged in a limestone cliff, and is believed to have carried a crew of ten or more humanoids. It's rumored there were even survivors of the crash and that, for years, around 2000 BCE, they lived within the canyon near the crash site. Ancient cave paintings are said to confirm this, as they consist of drawings of humanoid creatures with "bulbous" heads.

UFO historians claim a team of scientists, part of a joint military task force, according to various UFO watchdog websites, was brought to the bottom of the Grand Canyon to identify the debris. It's said the space vehicle was found in relatively good condition, considering its advanced age. The discovery of the crash and its subsequent investigation were quickly hidden from public view, according to many conspiracies, in a move similar to the alleged Roswell UFO crash from 1947.

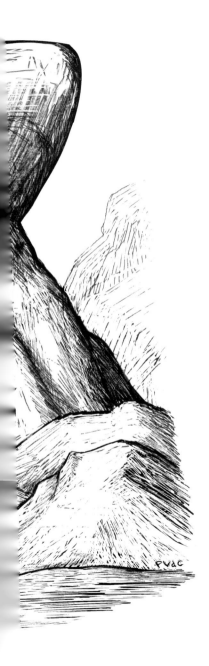

The story, due to its age and the vastness of the Grand Canyon, is difficult to confirm, but that doesn't stop true believers from insisting the event should be included in the ongoing history of UFO visits. Enthusiasts continue to analyze satellite imagery and discuss the incident on internet message boards.

This hasn't been the only UFO sighting at Grand Canyon, of course. Odd, colorful lights have been witnessed in the skies there over the years. What those odd lights and objects in the atmosphere are is anyone's guess. In more recent years, stories of those sightings have made their way to the internet in even greater numbers. A YouTube video posted in 2021 by Only Real UFOs, for instance, showed a mysterious object passing through the walls of the Grand Canyon in the middle of the day. A helicopter can also be heard in the background of the fourteen-minute-long video, and it is later seen as well. What the mysterious object is, whether it was a lost balloon or a craft from another world, remains to be seen.

The channel Unveiled also posted a video alleging the existence of an alien portal at the Grand Canyon. Citing the canyon as a perfect way for otherworldly beings to travel from one place to another, the video suggests that one or more of these "gateways" are located at the natural wonder. The portal story cited several examples of where these portals are and how they work, and it says that they may be connected to another dimension. The

Did an unidentified flying object crash near Grand Canyon's Commanche Point four thousand years ago? And were there alien survivors of that crash? *Illustration by Paul Van de Carr.*

website Medium, alluding to these portals, featured a mysterious cavern in a November 2023 story. The cavern, it alleged, is known only to a select few individuals. The underground cavern is expansive, according to the story, and exudes an aura. It's rumored that those who discover the area and unlock its secrets are bestowed with vast knowledge. Some have connected the cavern to UFO reports from the 1950s and hinted at the possibility there could be an alien base somewhere within the canyon itself.

Native tribes have a rich oral tradition that includes stories of the "star people" or "sky beings." According to these legends, shared among the Lakota, Cherokee and others, these celestial entities have interacted with Native ancestors and continue to influence Native lives. The star people are considered divine beings and are said to have played a vital role in the creation of the world, according to Native tradition. It's said these celestial visitors instructed the tribe in the ways of agriculture, spirituality and the interconnectedness of all lifeforms. The star people are referred to as the guardians of the Earth.

12

SNOWFLAKE

The Eerie, Famous Abduction

When you think of the word *snowflake*, you probably think of fluffy bits of ice falling from the sky on a cold, dark night. For most, it equates to the idea of hot cocoa and a warm fire. When you think of Snowflake, Arizona, however, and its location in the White Mountains, the vision changes. You think less of Christmasy notions and more of almond-shaped eyes and gray flesh, cold metal probes and blinding bursts of light. Snowflake, Arizona, for those who know about its past, conjures thoughts of aliens.

Snowflake was founded in 1878 by pioneers William Jordan Flake and Erastus Snow, both members of the Mormon Church. Flake, a skilled farmer, made his way to the Little Colorado River Valley in the hopes of establishing a community there. Snow himself was a member of the Quorum of the Twelve Apostles in the Church of Jesus Christ of Latter-day Saints. And their two names together? The town's namesake. The two were part of a larger Mormon effort to move away from areas where they faced hostility and persecution. Church leader Jesse N. Smith also contributed significantly to the town's religious and civic life.

William Jordan Flake was born in North Carolina in 1839. He moved west with the Mormon pioneer migration to Utah in the 1850s. He founded the town of Snowflake with a group of other settlers, including his brother James Madison Flake and Snow. Flake's farming prowess proved invaluable. With his help, the community erected an irrigation system and prepped the land for crops and livestock.

Mormon Erastus Snow, an apostle of the faith in the Mormon Church, is considered one of the religion's first emissaries of the Old West. His task? To oversee the settlement of Mormon colonies throughout the western territories and help gather and supply both support and resources for Mormon settlers.

Flake and Snow worked hard to build the community in a sustainable fashion. When they first stepped foot in the Little Colorado River Valley, they realized the terrain would be a challenge due to the area's harsh weather conditions, limited water and Native tribal members who didn't welcome strangers. Despite these setbacks, they established schools and other city organizations.

Popular attractions in the city include the James Madison Flake Home and the Jesse N. Smith Memorial Home. Annual Snowflake events include Pioneer Days and the Red Rock Lavender Festival. Nearby attractions, such as the Painted Desert National Park and the Sunrise Park Ski Resort, offer plenty to do for the whole family.

The town, approximately 175 miles north of Phoenix, would become known to UFO enthusiasts, or ufologists, much later.

For that, we have to travel to November 1975, a time when disco ruled and a quart of milk cost about fifty cents, a time before Spielberg filmed *E.T. the Extra-Terrestrial* and long after Snow and Flake had left their mark in the community of Snowflake.

The alleged abduction of logger Travis Walton near Snowflake is one of the most infamous stories of abduction in the annals of ufology. Walton claimed he was abducted by extraterrestrial beings on November 5, 1975, while working in the Apache-Sitgreaves National Forest. The national forest, located in eastern Arizona, covers more than two million acres and includes harsh mountains and gorgeous meadows. Human habitation in the area dates back thousands of years. Natives, including the Apache, inhabited these lands for centuries. The forests provided wildlife for hunting and the means for gathering nuts and other provisions, not to mention the basics needed for crafting tools, baskets and ceremonial items.

European settlers, attracted by the area's ranching, logging and mining opportunities, wouldn't begin to surface there in large numbers until the 1800s, particularly during the silver rush of 1870. Conservation efforts would begin in the late 1800s to preserve the area's natural beauty and not drain it completely for future generations.

Some of the most notable features of the Apache-Sitgreaves National Forest are the ponderosa pines, Douglas firs and aspens. Its wildlife includes elk, deer, black bears, mountain lions and more. The presence of this flora and fauna is due to the diverse habitats that are found in the forest: high-elevation forests, riparian areas and alpine meadows, all of which make life plentiful.

The Apache-Sitgreaves National Forest is home to archaeological sites, which offer ancient petroglyphs, ruins and other Native artifacts. Today, the area is known for its outdoor recreation, hiking, camping, fishing, hunting and beautiful landscapes. It's also known for Travis Walton.

According to testimonies from the incident, Walton and his coworkers had finished work that November day and were driving home. The group hadn't gotten far when they observed a saucer-shaped object in the sky above the tree line. Walton alone approached the craft, according to reports. And when he did, he was immediately captured by an intense beam of light. Walton later indicated that the light knocked him unconscious. His coworkers drove away when Walton was struck by the beam but returned when they saw the saucer drive away. By then, Walton had disappeared.

According to Walton's account, he awoke to find himself on board the alien spacecraft, which is when the true horror began.

Marking the forty-year anniversary of the abduction in 2015, Walton was featured in an article for the *White Mountain Independent* written by Karen Warnick. "They forced me down on the table, but I lost consciousness, and the next thing I remember is waking up on a highway."

Travis Walton's alien abduction, an ordeal chronicled in the 1993 movie *Fire in the Sky*, made national news when it occurred in November 1975. *Illustration by Jason McLean.*

Walton's disappearance, meanwhile, led to a five-day search effort that involved local law enforcement, a volunteer posse and the national guard. They found no sign of him. But on November 10, Walton reappeared, a bit confused and weary, near Heber-Overgaard, Arizona. He was quick to share his story.

Walton's dramatic reappearance made national news, with newspapers and television stations across the country reporting on his otherworldly allegations. Two years later, in 1978, he penned the book *The Walton Experience*, in which he provided an in-depth description of his time aboard the UFO. Certain copies of the original book fetch over $500 from hardcore buyers. Current editions of the book are available on Walton's personal website, travis-walton.com, at a much more affordable price.

While there are those who have expressed their doubts about the story, citing inconsistencies in his account and suggesting the encounter was made up to garner fame and fortune, a result of a hallucination or other reasons, Walton himself never backed down from the claim. Over the years, he made appearances on AZ Central and MSNBC and in a host of UFO-related documentaries.

Walton's wild claims were, nearly twenty years later, adapted into the 1993 film *Fire in the Sky*. Directed by Robert Lieberman, the film starred D.B. Sweeney as Travis and remained close to the book's depiction of Walton's alleged ordeal, though select details were altered, according to Walton himself. The film received mixed reviews from critics but has since become a cult classic among UFO enthusiasts.

According to the website UFO Sightings USA, Arizona is a hot spot for extraterrestrial sightings, ranking number seven in the nation among states with the highest number of reports. According to that website's data, 4,947 reported UFO sightings were shared in Arizona between the years 1969 and 2024. The city with the most UFO sightings is, of course, Phoenix, perhaps because of our next otherworldly story.

13

PHOENIX

Invasion of the Phoenix Lights

It was an Arizona evening that will go down in infamy.

On March 13, 1997, thousands of people in Phoenix, Arizona, and across the state witnessed one of the most famous and perplexing UFO sightings in history, known today as the Phoenix lights. Next to the abduction case from up north near Snowflake, it is the most notorious mass sighting in the state's history. And the sighting wasn't just restricted to Arizona. Reports also came in from Nevada.

Around 7:30 p.m., on a clear spring evening, reports to Phoenix emergency services and media outlets began to pour in. Eyewitnesses claimed to see the same things, describing in detail what others had also witnessed. Strange glowing lights moved like a whisper across the blanket of night, attached to what could best be described as a massive "V" formation and spanning what witnesses believed to be miles of airspace. The lights were said to have two smaller lights on each arm, with one light at the center where the arms were joined. Unlike in other sightings across the state, Phoenix witnesses claimed they saw stationary lights as well. Video footage of the strange occurrence blanketed the local news channels, such as Fox 10 News, that evening. Some said there were at least ten strange craft involved in the incident. While UFOs have been more recently referred to as UAP (or unidentified aerial phenomenon), the term *UFO* is still the most commonly used when describing these unexplainable craft.

Even actor Kurt Russell reported seeing strange objects while flying his private plane into Phoenix with his longtime partner Goldie Hawn's son

While centered primarily over the Valley of the Sun, the Phoenix lights were seen as far away as Prescott. To this day, the incident remains one of the largest UFO sightings in history. *Public domain photo.*

Oliver Hudson that fateful evening. Russell, in interviews, said he identified bright lights in the sky and radioed the control tower to file a report. It's estimated that tens of thousands viewed the lights—and not just for a few minutes but for several hours. Reports came in from as far away as Tucson and Mexico as well, and all reported details like what was observed in Phoenix. Another celebrity who witnessed the event is famous rocker Alice Cooper, who lives in the Phoenix metro area.

The air force initially claimed the lights were the result of flares dropped by A-10 Warthog aircraft during a training exercise. The military was participating in what has become known as Operation Snowbird, a pilot training program. Those who witnessed the lights insist the sighting couldn't merely be flares, however, or even military aircraft, due to the sheer size of the craft they observed. Alien theorists believe earthbound experimental craft would have been heard as well, while the Phoenix Lights ran silently. The stationary lights that were also seen above Phoenix were said to be part of the same military exercise, in which A-10 jets dropped flares. The exercise was run through Davis-Monthan Air Force Base in Tucson.

From 1997 to 2008, coast-to-coast reports of mysterious lights, strange objects and unexplained phenomena flooded news agencies. The National UFO Reporting Center, according to its records, received over ten thousand reports of UFO sightings from individuals across the country in 1997 alone. And in 2008, approximately eleven years after the Phoenix lights, Phoenix residents found their city the object of otherworldly attention yet again.

Commonly referred to as Phoenix lights 2.0, the incident, which occurred on April 21, 2008, closely mirrored the flyover of 1997. Witnesses reported seeing a series of bright lights that formed a linear pattern and

Hollywood legend Kurt Russell is among those who witnessed the Phoenix lights in 1997. Russell piloted his personal plane into the valley that evening and radioed in a report of the sighting. *Illustration by Jason McLean.*

hovered above the evening sky, just like what they had seen in 1997. These eyewitnesses accounts described white and orange lights and sometimes red lights, this time arranged in a straight line or diamond-shaped pattern, which appeared to progress in a coordinated manner. Reports said the lights would appear and then vanish. In any event, the lights were visible for several minutes. In a *Live Science* article, journalist Benjamin Radford explained, however, that a local man had come forward to declare he tied road flares to balloons to play a prank on the community. Despite the admission, doubters disregard the implication that the incident was a hoax and instead look to the stars for an answer.

Whatever these lights may have been, they have helped flag Phoenix as an alleged hotbed for UFO activity.

In the years following the original Phoenix lights, UFO sightings continued across the United States. One story came from Chicago, where thousands of people witnessed strange red lights flying above them. Known as the Tinley Park lights, the incident occurred on Halloween night 2004, and thanks to the advent of the smartphone, it was observed, photographed and filmed.

Another Chicago-based sighting occurred in November 2006, when several airline pilots reported a mysterious, saucer-shaped UFO hovering over Gate C-17.

And in 2008, prior to the second Phoenix sighting, residents of Stephenville, Texas, reported a massive, silent object hovering over the community, and this time, there were military jets in pursuit. The incident described a boomerang-shaped craft, like the one seen in Phoenix. Some also described it as being shaped like a Dorito chip. The incident is popular among ufologists and was even featured on the Netflix show *Encounters*.

Sightings weren't only an American pastime between 1997 and 2008; they were popular in other countries as well. In 2005 in Canada, witnesses in St. Stephen, New Brunswick, claimed they saw a series of bright, multicolored lights moving erratically in the night sky.

Triangular UFOs are a recurring theme in the modern world, unlike past descriptions that indicate a round saucer shape. In 1989, for instance, a large triangular craft was observed in the sky over Eupen, a community in Belgium near the German border. Over the course of days, numerous Belgians reported seeing the same thing: a large triangular craft or platform, sometimes seen with one large red light or multiple lights.

Other countries also experienced their share of UFO sightings during this same twenty-year period, including Africa, Asia, France, Australia and elsewhere.

UFO sightings have also been reported in France, Australia, Brazil, Argentina and Chile. Residents of Buenos Aires in 2002 reported a large, saucer-shaped object hovering over the city for several minutes before it disappeared into the night. It, too, was caught on camera.

So, what is happening across the world? Are these visitations from another world, as believers insist, or are they something else? Theories on UFOs come from several sources, which include astronomists, physicists, psychologists and of course ufologists. While theorists seek to explain UFO sightings as natural or manufactured phenomena, others propose more unconventional rationalizations, from alien encounters to covert government cover-ups.

Called the extraterrestrial hypothesis (ETH), this theory posits these crafts are piloted by intelligent beings from other worlds. ETH proponents believe the magnitude of reported encounters serves as all the evidence needed to prove aliens have been among us. Famous historical sightings, such as 1947's crash in Roswell, are often cited as proof of the cover-ups.

A second notion theorizes that UFOs could be advanced military aircraft or experimental corporate technology. This idea grew in popularity during the

Sightings of strange lights in the night sky were reported in Sedona in 2012. Those strange lights, it turns out, like other reports, were confirmed to be from a remotely operated drone. *Illustration by Jason McLean.*

Cold War between the Soviet Union and the United States. These triangular aircraft, or black triangles, have often been attributed to classified military projects. Accusations of government cover-ups about UFO sightings have persisted for decades. Recent declassified documents, such as those released by the Central Intelligence Agency (CIA) and the United States Air Force, have added fuel to the fire when it comes to those claiming the government knew of UFOs all along.

Drones and other unmanned aerial vehicles (UAVs) are these days often mistaken for alien spacecraft. Everyone has access to a drone or remotely operated apparatus, which has resulted in an increase in reported UFO sightings. In Sedona, for instance, in 2012, residents called local news reporters to report strange lights in the sky near the Village of Oak Creek. But those lights turned out to be an early version of a drone.

Psychological theories take another route. They suggest that UFO sightings could stem from misperceptions, hallucinations or factors like sleep paralysis and hypnagogic and hypnopompic (transitioning to or from sleep) hallucinations. Some say suggestibility may play into the theory that it's all in the head. Pop culture experts suggest that media, movies, cartoons and video games contribute to the belief in UFOs, making it easy to misinterpret something unidentifiable in the atmosphere.

Then there are the amateur meteorologists. UFO debunkers bring up natural explanations, such as atmospheric phenomena like ball lightning, meteors and other anomalies, which can create optical illusions under the right circumstances. Those other anomalies can include temperature inversions and atmospheric refraction, which distort the appearance of objects in the sky and make them appear otherworldly.

Those who insist on the existence of those otherworldly visitors, however, need merely point to the events of Roswell, New Mexico, as an example of the reality of aliens.

Roswell is the most famous out-of-this-world encounter of all time, bigger than the *Fire in the Sky* incident and the Phoenix lights. Roswell, located in New Mexico about 275 miles southeast of Flagstaff, played a large part in the current flying saucer craze that remains to this day.

Around July 7, 1947, it's said an alien craft crash landed on a ranch owned by rancher William "Mac" Brazel. Brazel, when he investigated the scene, came across scattered debris. This included fragments of metal, an odd foil-like material and other unusual items. He reported the discovery to local authorities, who contacted officials at the Roswell Army Airfield (RAAF). Roswell Army Airfield was home to the 509th Bomb Group, at that time the only atomic bomb squadron in the world.

While officials with RAAF originally issued a press release stating they had recovered a flying disc, that statement was retracted the next day. Instead, the officials claimed the recovered material was the remains of a lost weather balloon with an attached radar for atmospheric study.

At the time, the story of the Roswell crash faded into obscurity, but it wouldn't stay that way. By the 1970s, interest in UFO crashes had exploded. Extraterrestrial researchers published books, journalists started deep investigations that included witness interviews and UFO enthusiasts leaned in to hear every word spoken about the Roswell story. Many of these books questioned the validity of the weather balloon statement, and any of the subsequent stories instead insisted that an alien ship had come to a permanent, deadly end on American soil, and some accused the United States government of secretly recovering the wreckage.

One witness helped fuel that belief. Jesse Marcel, an air force intelligence officer, said he managed the debris from the crash. He went on to indicate the material found at the ranch wasn't consistent with that of a weather balloon. Other recovered items, he added, showed signs of advanced technology.

The incident has proven to have everlasting appeal when it comes to pop culture. Books, movies and television shows, including a show named *Roswell*, have all capitalized on the public's fascination with the 1947 crash.

14

TUCSON

Strange Sightings in the Sky

Readers may remember the Warthog aircraft mentioned in the prior chapter when it was revealed as a possible explanation for the Phoenix lights. Those planes can be found in ample supply approximately two hours south of Phoenix, toward the border with Mexico, at Davis-Monthan Air Force Base (DM AFB). It's one of the reasons people look toward the sky in Tucson. But not everything they see comes from Earth.

Established in 1925, DM AFB has played a crucial role in national defense, training and aerospace research. Originally named Tucson Field, or Davis-Monthan Landing Field, the large base served as a refueling stop for military aircraft making their way between the East and West Coasts. The base, in 1925, was designated Davis-Monthan Field in honor of two men: Lieutenants Samuel H. Davis and Oscar Monthan, both of whom lost their lives in different aviation accidents.

Davis-Monthan Field expanded during World War II to accommodate growing military demands, and it served as a training site for bomber crews. The base also provided support for aerial reconnaissance missions, not to mention testing of new aircraft and other technologies.

After the war ended, Davis-Monthan was used as a storage and maintenance facility for the 309th Aerospace Maintenance and Regeneration Group's (AMARG) surplus military aircraft. The desert landscape surrounding the base provided more than enough space for aircraft storage. Thousands of retired and decommissioned aircraft were eventually stored at Davis-Monthan, and it began to be called the Boneyard. The aircraft storage yard,

Warthog aircraft, said to have been in operation during the Phoenix lights event (*pictured*), fly out of Davis-Monthan Air Force Base in Tucson. *Illustration by Jason McLean.*

which features a vast landscape of large, decommissioned planes was even featured in one of the *Transformers* movies in later years. It's thought to be the largest aircraft storage and preservation facility in the world and is home to thousands of retired aircraft from all branches of the U.S. military.

By 1948, the base was renamed again to Davis-Monthan Air Force Base and was handed over to the newly established United States Air Force, formed in 1947 from of the National Security Act, which created the Department of the Air Force.

Davis-Monthan Air Force Base is now home to the 355th Wing, which controls a fleet of A-10 Thunderbolt IIs, commonly known by the rugged Warthog moniker. The A-10 is designed to provide ground forces with air support during combat. Besides that, the 355th Wing also conducts combat search and rescue missions, intelligence operations, surveillance and humanitarian and reconnaissance missions, according to the Davis-Monthan Air Force Base's website.

In addition to the Warthog, sky watchers can see a variety of other aircraft in the area, including fighter jets, cargo planes and helicopters while on training missions or participating in airshows and more. As a bustling center for flights and aviation, Tucson is no stranger to its share of aviation disasters, including a crash that occurred just days before Christmas 1967. On Monday December 18, 1967, at 5:44 p.m., a U.S. Air Force Phantom Jet plummeted from the air, crashing into a grocery store and killing four people. The store was located at 1830 South Alvernon Street. News accounts at the time indicated it was a miracle more people weren't killed in the crash, as a handful of holiday shoppers were present at the time of the tragedy.

Twelve years after the grocery store catastrophe, another jet crashed into Tucson. The incident occurred shortly after noon on October 26, 1978, when an A-7D Corsair II jet encountered engine trouble. The pilot aimed the plane toward the University of Arizona's (UA) football field before parachuting to safety. While the field would normally have been an ideal landing location, the ditched plane never made it there. Instead, it crashed into a street. One person was killed.

From hosting military craft to commercial and private planes departing from Tucson International Airport, the skies over this part of the state are never boring.

Outside of the Phoenix Metropolitan area, Tucson International serves as the main airport for Pima County. Airlines like American Airlines, Delta Air Lines and Southwest Airlines operate regular flights out of Tucson. The city is home to general aviation airports and private airfields as well, those catering to private and corporate aircraft owners. Ryan Airfield (RYN) and Marana Regional Airport (AVW) are among the airports in the vicinity of Tucson. According to their websites, these smaller airports support a range of aircraft, from single-engine propeller planes to corporate jets and helicopters.

One of the earliest documented UFO sightings in Tucson occurred in 1949, just after 5:30 p.m. on April 28. Three men, including a well-known florist, spotted a sliver object hovering over the Catalina Mountains. While the sighting lasted a total of twelve minutes, all three witnesses described the same thing: a craft with no wings or visible openings at all. At the time, the florist noted, "It appeared sausage-like in shape."

The so-called sausage was said to revolve and reached an estimated speed of about five hundred miles per hour. It's said it reached an altitude between five and ten miles up.

On April 3, 1952, another notable alien encounter occurred near Marana, just outside Tucson on the way north to Phoenix. A flying instructor had just landed at the airfield at 7:45 a.m. when he noticed what he called a "bright star" in the sky. "It never moved the slightest fraction in relation to the canopy of my aircraft," he reported. "The object was bright and shone like polished aluminum. I've been flying for 25 years and never saw anything like it. It was weird." He observed the object for a total of forty-five minutes before it finally disappeared.

Further back in 1972, there was a report of a Tucson triangle that "emitted dread." The incident was observed on November 8 that year at around 8:00 p.m. The object in the sky, seen near David-Monthan, was described as flat black object with a bright light that shimmered around the edges. The craft was alleged to have shot out a beam of light that raised the dust in front of those who witnessed it. The beam, it's said, was strong enough to kick up dust when it hit the ground. Not only that, but when the beam hit the ground, eyewitnesses indicated that a feeling of dread and nauseousness came over them. As the incident occurred near the base, military personnel seemed to go on alert as well. Sirens and security staff could be heard and seen following the incident.

The "mirror over a mountain" was observed on September 18, 2013, at approximately 11:00 p.m. According to testimony from the National UFO Reporting Center (NUFORC), three truck drivers were traveling on Interstate 10 when they saw the object, described as a saucer-shaped craft that shone like a giant mirror reflecting the sun. The truck drivers alleged that fighter jets emerged over a mountain and headed toward the craft, only for the object to rise and shoot straight up into the atmosphere, where it disappeared. The mirror craft was thought to be at least forty-eight feet in diameter.

These are only a sampling of the sightings witnessed in Arizona, a handful with rational explanations and some that are hard to explain, leading many to surmise these objects may have been ships piloted by creatures that appear nothing like us.

Of course, sightings in southern Arizona aren't just restricted to Tucson. The small town of Bisbee, a couple of hours from Tucson, is not immune to alien visitation. A video posted to YouTube indicated an incident occurred in 2023. On June 24 that year, the witness shot footage of a white craft passing over the community in the middle of the day, though the object itself is hard to make out. It was described as a round object with flashing colored lights that passed over the Mule Mountains.

Ufologists question why aliens look the way they do. This can be due to numerous reasons, including evolutionary theories stemming from the differences of gravity and even their advanced evolutionary appearances. Cosmic life may be further along the evolutionary ladder than us humans.

Evolution may also hold the answer to why alien eyes are different than human eyes. They're often described as being much larger than human eyes, black and almond shaped. Living on a different planet might mean the amount of light they receive is different than what we get on Earth, leading them to need bigger eyes to retain more of that light. Their smaller size, as well, may be due to quite a few factors related to their origins. Often, they're described as being smaller than humans, and this may be due to the physical environment they evolved in. Descriptions in modern, pulp-fiction and science fiction stories have also, albeit inadvertently, influenced how we perceive aliens. Questions remain for many of these encounters. Believers insist life exists beyond our own atmosphere and say it is only a matter of time before they make their presence widely known, while others are of the opinion that these sightings have a more down-to-Earth explanation.

But even earthly creatures can often defy explanation, as we'll see when we explore cryptids in the following chapters.

PART IV

CREEPY CRYPTIDS

15

GRAND CANYON

What Is the Mogollon Monster?

The Mogollon (pronounced mo-gee-on) Rim lies across a vast section of northern and central Arizona, approximately two hundred miles north of Yavapai County and across into New Mexico. Known as an escarpment, or a long cliff, the Rim outlines the southwestern boundaries of the Colorado Plateau, which sprawls across the Four Corners region of the Southwest. The Rim is a popular destination for outdoor enthusiasts thanks to its spectacular forest views and cliffs formed in sandstone and limestone. The picturesque locale has become well known for its hiking, exploration and geological features. The land's sedimentary, volcanic and metamorphic rock date to the Precambrian era. The Mogollon Rim is adorned with dramatic cliffs, high elevations and inspiring pine forests. Its elevation ranges from four thousand feet above sea level to approximately eight thousand feet above sea level.

Lakes and creeks, such as Bear Canyon Lake and Woods Canyon Lake, offer plentiful fishing, and due to the surrounding forests, hunters from all over the state are drawn to the area as well. Rim Lake Vista Trail and Kinder Crossing Trail, along with numerous others, offer beautiful views and adventure for hikers. Cabins and outdoor camping sites can be found throughout the Rim. Ponderosa Pine Forest covers a great deal of the land there. *Pinus ponderosa* is a large coniferous pine, and while it's the official state tree of Montana, the ponderosa can be found in abundance along the Mogollon Rim. Other species of trees found throughout the Rim include aspen and maple trees.

A family looks over the picturesque Mogollon Rim, the home of the burly Mogollon Monster, in this photograph from 1958. The rim covers the Colorado Plateau's southwestern boundaries. *USDA Forest Service.*

Interstate 17 cuts through the Mogollon Rim as it travels north from Phoenix to Flagstaff. Arizona cities found along the Rim include Sedona, Pine Top–Lakeside and Payson.

While the Mogollon Rim offers plenty for travelers and locals, it's also home to a great deal of wildlife. Peregrine falcons, which nest along the cliffs, share the airspace with a variety of birds, including swallows, thrushes and different warbler species. Bald eagles can also be seen regularly. Many of the area's federally listed species—such as the southwestern willow flycatcher, the Mexican spotted owl and the Chiracahua leopard frog—make their home in the Mogollon Rim.

Bigger animals dwell in the area as well, including elk and deer, not to mention assorted black bears, which can be seen patrolling their territories. Coyotes are also plentiful in the area. Elk, one of the largest members of the deer family, *Cervidae*, are characterized by the white fur on their rump. Male elk, which grow large antlers that they shed annually, and cow elk are frequent sights in northern Arizona. They differ from deer, such as mule deer, which can also be found in the Mogollon Rim, by their size. Male elk also grow antlers from the top of their head, while deer do not. Elk find their diet sated in the Mogollon Rim due to a steady supply of grasses and shrubs, and they are known as a grazing species, unlike deer, which are known as a browser species, meaning deer eat from bushes and leaves primarily.

Black bears can be found throughout the state of Arizona but tend to dwell in Chaparral pine forests and aspen fir pine forests. Male black bears can weigh up to 350 pounds, while females can weigh up to 250 pounds.

Bear cubs are typically born in January in pairs, though there are sometimes larger litters. They typically don't emerge from their den until April. Black bears are the most commonly found bear in North America and can be seen in thirty-eight states. Black bears are considered extremely intelligent and curious creatures. As omnivores, black bears can be attracted to any number of food sources, including those found in the Mogollon Rim and even in areas populated by people. They prefer forested regions, however.

Another lesser-known resident of the Mogollon Rim that is even larger than a black bear or an elk is the Mogollon Monster. Standing at over seven feet tall and believed to have glowing red or green eyes, the Mogollon Monster is a bigfoot-like creature that is thought to call the Mogollon Rim home. Also known as the Arizona Bigfoot, the Mogollon Monster has been described as a being covered in fur that is ape-like in appearance.

The creature is believed to be an omnivore, eating both plants and meat. It's also bipedal, walking on two legs, and is thought to be nocturnal. While it is rumored to mimic the sounds of other animals to blend in, its screams have been widely reported, and the call is said to chill the blood when heard. They're also believed to hurl stones at those who get too close to them and have been said to be violent, even decapitating deer with sheer brute force. While sightings of the creature have been reported as far south as Prescott and Williams, many associate the Mogollon Monster with the Grand Canyon area, where one of the earliest sightings was said to occur.

Footprints of the creature, according to *Weird Arizona* author Wesley Treat, have been measured at twenty-two inches in length. The monster is said to have a long stride, with long, almost uncanny steps.

In 1903, the *Williams News* and *Arizona Republic* newspapers ran a story about an encounter between Cedar, Colorado hunter I.W. Stevens and the Mogollon Monster near Grand Canyon. Stevens described the creature as a being covered in gray and white hair with a matted beard and bare spots that revealed "dirty skin" beneath. Its face, he said, was "seared and burned brown by the sun." The creature wore no clothing and had a long beard that reached down to its knees. According to the account Stevens provided, the encounter occurred when he came upon the creature after disembarking from his boat. He stopped after observing large footprints in a sandbar along the water's edge and wanted to investigate what had made such large tracks. When the creature saw Stevens, it threatened him with a club and began screeching at him. Stevens recounted that he nearly fired at the creature but instead shot a mountain lion that was also approaching the two. The monster fled, and Stevens returned to his boat—but not

The hairy Mogollon Monster is estimated to stand over seven feet tall with glowing red or green eyes and is described as walking on two legs but in an apelike fashion. *Illustration by Paul Van de Carr.*

before he noticed the monster had come back to feast with talon-like claws on the mountain lion and the two cubs it had in tow.

Another incident occurred near Payson in 1944, when Don Davis took part in an innocent camping trip with a Boy Scouts group. Davis was awoken by the creature raiding the campsite and observed it while hiding in his sleeping bag. He described the monster as being huge, with no hair on its face and dark, inset eyes that seemed expressionless. The creature's chest, shoulders and arms were massive, according to this account. Besides the face, Davis described the cryptid as being nearly covered in thick hair.

Davis, a self-described cryptozoologist, added, "The face/head was very square; square sides and squared up chin, like a box."

Another incident near Payson occurred more recently when a twenty-eight-year-old female sociology student reported a sighting after hiking in the area. Her account described the creature as "troll-like," covered in grayish hair with bumpy-skinned face, bulbous nose and dark, reddish eyes. She encountered the creature as it was drinking from a pool of water. When it noticed her, the creature fled, running like a human on two legs, and it moved too quickly for her to take a photograph, according to the testimony. Like Davis, the woman described the creature as expressionless. "It was on its knees, drinking water, when I found it. Drinking, making noises like a pig, so at first sight the animal looked like a pig to me," she reported to *Cryptozoology News*.

Like in bigfoot encounters, witnesses have often described detecting a foul stench before seeing the Mogollon Monster. The stench is described as being skunky or smelling like a dead fish. Often, an eerie stillness is described as well, of the sort where wildlife, birds and smaller animals go silent when the presence of a predatory animal is nearby.

In 2006, White Mountain Apache Nation Tribal Police lieutenant Ray Burnette reported that, for years, residents have reported encounters that match the description of the Mogollon Monster. The Fort Apache Indian Reservation is located along the border of Arizona and New Mexico. The reservation is situated in areas of the Navajo, Apache and Gila Counties. Burnette cited a number of incidents in which residents of the rural community called the police, terrified, to report that dark, hairy beasts were peeking into their windows.

There are Native beliefs behind the identity of the Mogollon Monster, which some tribes have nicknamed "the old man of the mountain," including a prehistoric tale of an exiled tribal chief. The chief, in ill regard for the tribe that banished him, prayed to become their "boogeyman," forever haunting their lands in the form of the hairy, violent beast. Another tale holds that a rival stole the chief's wife. Out of revenge, he instructed his traditional healer to transform the thief into the monster. Other legends say the Mogollon Monster is the cursed spirit of a pioneer who murdered a Native woman. The pioneer was strung up in a tree, skinned alive and left to die. The hanging stretched his arms, making him appear ape-like, and the spirits condemned him to live forever as a horrid, rampaging beast. Yet another belief states the pioneer escaped into the woods, where he went insane and turned feral from the effects of the curse.

No matter the stories, tales of the Mogollon Monster continue. A website was even created to collect data and accounts from eyewitnesses to discover

Some believe this artist's rendering of a sacred site of the Yokuts of the Tule River tribe of the Tule River Reservation in Tulare County, California, is remarkably like descriptions of the Mogollon Monster. Others think it shows a family of Bigfoots. *Public domain.*

the truth behind the elusive cryptid. Created by the late Mitchell Waite, MogollonMonster.com is no longer an active website since his passing as of late 2023. Waite was featured on news programs, and videos of him discussing the Mogollon Monster can still be viewed on YouTube. His partner, writer Susan Farnsworth, in 2011, authored a book on the legendary cryptid, *The Mogollon Monster, Arizona's Bigfoot.*

In 2008, another cryptozoologist, Alex Hearn, described an encounter he had with the Mogollon Monster near Young, Arizona. Hearn has reported two encounters with the creature in all. His 2008 encounter, however, occurred just off Highway 288, where he saw the creature covered in what he described as reddish-brown fur, walking bolt upright and moving branches out of its path as it pushed through the forest. He said he made eye contact before the creature moved on. He'd encounter another creature not much later while investigating the White Mountain Apache Nation sightings. His group approached a campground, he reported, when they all heard ear-splitting screams from the forest. While investigating the sounds, he said the creature appeared from behind a tree approximately twenty feet away from him. He described this creature as being smaller than the other. Thermal imagers used by other members of the group alerted Hearn to the presence of yet another creature, though both quickly disappeared.

Art and imagery, including podcasts, featuring the Mogollon beast, can be found throughout popular culture. The creature's rugged, hairy likeness can be found on everything from T-shirts to phone holders. A trail race, The Mogollon Monster 100 in Pine, has been named after the creature, and large wooden sculptures have been made to honor the creature's presence, whether real or not, along the Mogollon Rim.

16

Navajo Nation

The Story of the Skinwalkers

What is a cryptid anyway?

The standard definition of a cryptid is that it is an animal stemming from folklore or mythology that persists in the modern world. These cryptids are considered real, and like the skinwalkers of this chapter, they strike terror in the hearts of those who believe in them. This can be due to a belief in creatures based on a religion or due to unexplainable modern-day sightings from eyewitnesses that range from law enforcement to the neighbors across the street. Of course, they can also instill primal fear in those who happen to run afoul of one, whether they have heard of them before or not.

While there are hundreds, if not thousands, of cryptids and firsthand accounts of cryptid encounters, the legend of the wendigo is one of the most famous in North American folklore and is even up there with bigfoot. The wendigo is believed to be a malevolent spirit that inhabits forested regions of both Canada and the northern section of the United States. Algonquian legend states the wendigo is a Hulk-sized supernatural being with an insatiable appetite for human flesh. The wendigo is said to possess its victims and force them to commit acts of cannibalism. The wendigo is still seen regularly by those who delve deep into the northern wilderness.

If the monstrous wendigo were to have siblings, the cryptid yeti would make a viable candidate for that distinction. Typically reported in the mountains of Nepal, the yeti is more commonly known as the abominable snowman, the scourge of the Himalayas. Generally portrayed as a large, ape-like creature with layers of white fur, the yeti is said to leave icy footprints when it travels. Sightings of the yeti are common in those high, frozen areas of Nepal. Despite many expeditions to uncover the truth of the yeti, there is no definitive proof of its existence.

The Australian cryptid known as the yowie would be the yeti's close cousin—or even a member of the same species. Said to dwell in the remote Outback, the yowie is a lumbering, ape-like creature with bright eyes and reddish-brown fur. Indigenous tribes have shared stories of such a creature for hundreds of years. In some areas, yowie sightings still occur. Queensland resident Dean Harrison encountered one in 1995 while returning to his home on Mount Tamborine. "In the darkness behind the swamp there was this noise, booming and guttural, it made my hair stand on end. On top of the noise, it was bipedal, [I] could hear it walking, treading through the swamp.…Then it starts to rip foliage out of the ground, and throw it through the air," he told the news site, 7NEWS.com.au.

Meanwhile, in Germany, we find the wolpertinger, which may be the closest thing Europe has to the North American legend of the skinwalker. The wolpertinger is rumored to be a hybrid of many different animals, with the body of a rabbit, antlers of a deer and wings of a bird. This cryptid is said to inhabit the Bavarian forests and feed on human travelers and hunters. Sightings of the wolpertinger continue to this day.

The "wild man," or almas, of Russian legend could be a blend of the legend of bigfoot and the skinwalker. Stories of the almas have persisted in the remote parts of the country for centuries. In parts of Siberia, the fur-covered ape-like creature is considered a guardian spirit by the Indigenous population.

This brings us to the Navajo Nation's skinwalkers.

The Navajo Nation comprises the largest Native reservation in the United States. It covers portions of Arizona, New Mexico and Utah. The nation covers approximately twenty-seven thousand square miles and takes up most of the Four Corners region of the southwestern United States. Their story spans thousands of years—and includes the stories of skinwalkers.

Estimated at a population of about 392,000, the Navajo Nation is one of the largest Native tribes in the country. The Navajo people are also known as the Diné. *Diné Bikéyah*, or "Navajoland," summers can be hot and dry, while winters can be harsh and are known for freezing temperatures and snowfall, particularly in the vast mountainous regions.

Sheep herding, rug weaving, tourism, energy production and agriculture make up a large part of the tribe's economy. The craftsmanship behind Navajo rugs, jewelry and pottery is revered throughout the world, though

This photograph, taken some time between 1930 and 1938, shows two Navajo shearing sheep. The animals' wool was used for rug weaving. *Bureau of Indian Affairs.*

the nation has suffered recent hardships as well. Unemployment has led to poverty in many areas, but economic development initiatives, infrastructure improvements and investments in healthcare and education projects are underway.

Notable leaders of the Navajo people include Chief Manuelito. Born around 1818, Manuelito is known as a military leader who defended the Navajo homeland during the Navajo Wars against the United States. After years of resistance, in 1868, he signed the Treaty of Bosque Redondo. This allowed the Navajo people to move back to their ancestral territory in the Four Corners area.

Born in 1820, Chief Barboncito also played a significant role in negotiating the Bosque Redondo Treaty. Barboncito remained committed to preserving Navajo culture and traditions. He also promoted peace and was known for his attempts to mediate between conflicting groups. The Navajo have faced numerous challenges throughout their long history, including forced relocation, efforts to absorb them into unfamiliar cultures and the appropriation of their lands. One of the most traumatic events in Navajo history is known as the Long Walk, during which thousands of Navajo men, women and children were forced to walk hundreds of miles to a reservation in eastern New Mexico in the 1860s. It's estimated that fifty-three such forced marches occurred between August 1864 and the end of 1866.

Like it is in most civilizations, religion is a central facet of Navajo culture, though that connection with history has been adapted to modern life. Ceremonies, such as the Blessingway and the Enemyway, are still performed to maintain harmony and balance in the world.

In Navajo mythology, Changing Woman is among the culture's worshipped deities. She is revered for her connection to fertility and the cycle of life. According to legend, Changing Woman is an important part of the Navajo creation belief. She is the mother of the twins Monster Slayer and Born for Water. Changing Woman is thought to be immortal and, like a phoenix, can be reborn repeatedly. She is considered a force of life for the tribe.

The Spider Woman, a Navajo deity known for her weaving, wisdom and protection, is another legendary character in Navajo mythology. According to legend, she was instrumental in the creation of the world and is revered as a protector of the Navajo people.

Skinwalkers are also a staple of Navajo culture and mythology and are arguably one of their most well-known and frightening legends to outsiders.

Skinwalkers, or *yee naaldlooshii* in Navajo, are witchcraft practitioners with the ability to shape-shift into various animal forms, according to legend. These beings, commonly considered cryptids, are believed to possess dark magic that allows them to transform. They're also associated with death, sickness and other dark fates. They're endowed with the ability to change into and behave like a variety of animals, including wolves, coyotes, owls and more.

Said to be malevolent in nature, skinwalkers allegedly possess exceptional speed, agility and strength. Like wizards in a fantasy novel, they're also believed to have some control of the weather and can call forth storms when needed. Then there is their ability to mimic human voices to lure unsuspecting victims. Their eyes, however, are anything but human. Skinwalkers are believed to have glowing red and/or yellow eyes. Despite skinwalkers also being seen as a sign of resilience, Navajo teachings warn against engaging with or acknowledging them, as doing so is believed to invite their malevolent influence into one's life.

Sightings of skinwalkers on the Navajo Reservation are common, though reports often shared only with others in the tribe and not reported to outside authorities. Often, animals that show aggression to humans and stand on their hind legs are suspected of being skinwalkers. Chilling accounts have been shared in YouTube documentaries and on Reddit.

The most famous skinwalker story hails from an area just past the Arizona border in the state of Utah. In 1996, Terry Sherman was walking his dogs on his ranch property when he saw what he first believed to be a wolf. He

Skinwalkers are thought to be as strong as bears but also fast and agile and able to mimic human speech. It's also believed they have a supernatural influence over the weather. *Illustration by Jason McLean.*

quickly realized the wolf was at least three times larger than a normal wolf and had a set of glowing red eyes. As he was armed, Sherman fired shots at the creature, which remained unfazed and blocked his path. Sherman fled and sold the property shortly thereafter. Similar incidents were reported by the new owners of the property, which is now known by the name Skinwalker Ranch. Besides skinwalkers, the 512-acre property is said to be cursed by UFO sightings, animal mutilations and other horrors.

The belief in skinwalkers was even used as a defense in a 1987 murder trial held in Flagstaff, following the murder of a forty-year-old Navajo woman named Sarah Saganitso. Her body was allegedly discovered mutilated behind Flagstaff Medical Center. George Abney, a former professor at Northern Arizona University, was arrested for the crime. The defense, however, insisted she was killed by nothing less than a skinwalker, due to evidence found at the scene. This evidence included a stick found lying across her throat and graveyard grass found near her truck. While Abney was originally found guilty of the crime, according to an *Atlas Obscura* article, he was acquitted a year later. While this story has been researched, it has since passed into the realm of skinwalker urban legend.

Sightings in the years since come from varying corners of the Navajo Nation, some involving animals that acted out of character and others involving odd figures with desperate, glowing eyes that are part animal and part human.

It's rumored that, like the Grand Canyon's UFO connections portals, also said to exist in Sedona, skinwalkers make use of these same gateways to travel undetected. One of those portals is said to exist in Upper Antelope Canyon, located on Navajo land. The area, in a slot canyon, is one of the most photogenic spots in the world. It's also dangerous due to the possibility of flash floods there.

Documentaries, books and television shows have explored the popularity of the skinwalker legends. Researchers from everywhere have conducted field investigations and gathered eyewitness testimony. However, the secretive nature of Navajo culture and the deeply ingrained taboos surrounding skinwalker lore present significant challenges to these efforts.

Movies and documentaries on the subject include the films *Skinwalker Ranch* (2013), *The Descent* (2005), *Skinwalker* (2021) and many more. There have been an assortment of books written on the subject as well, from the 2005 title *Hunt for the Skinwalker: Science Confronts the Unexplained at a Remote Ranch in Utah*, by Colm A. Kelleher; to book seven in Tony Hillerman's best-selling Leaphorn & Chee series titled *Skinwalkers*.

17

SEDONA

Bold Bigfoot Encounters

Sedona may be one of the most beautiful locations in the state of Arizona, but as we've learned, it's not immune to the stranger things that occupy legend and lore. Vortexes are common in Red Rock Country, but so are other topics bordering on the unknown—including Bigfoot.

Renowned for its hiking and natural beauty, nestled comfortably in the Coconino National Forest, Sedona (as explored in chapter 5) is well known for its portals, resorts and spas and mystical ambience. Wind, water and the march of time on the geography have helped shape the Sedona community, as well as the neighboring village of Oak Creek.

While the vortexes bring loads of people to the red rocks, another type of resident is also said to inhabit the area, one with more fur than you would expect from your average tourist. Sightings of bigfoot, or as believers refer to it, a bigfoot-like creature, have been reported in the area for decades, though not in the numbers seen from the Pacific Northwest, where bigfoot, also known as sasquatches, are believed to exist in considerable numbers. Sighting hot spots include British Columbia, Washington and Oregon. The word *sasquatch* comes from the Native people of the Pacific Northwest, the Salishan tribes, and is derived from the Halkomelem word *sásq'ets*, which roughly translates to means "wild man" or "hairy man."

Settlers to the area and Native peoples all offer similar accounts of an ape-like creature that is covered in fur and quite large. An account from the 1920s indicated the creature, seen in the Sedona region by a group of prospectors, was covered in fur and stood over seven feet tall. The group claimed the creature had a muscular build and long arms, again like an ape. According to their testimony, the creature watched them from a distance, hidden behind trees, before vanishing without a trace. The creatures are believed to have mastered the ability to blend into their environment, making sightings quite rare.

Since the prospector sighting, bigfoot has made a number of further appearances in Red Rock Country, including an encounter in the summer of 1989. According to the first account, a man was touring some property that was under construction near Red Canyon when he came across not one but a group of the creatures. They were described as all being close to nine feet tall and appeared agitated, as if they were guarding the property from intruders. The man, according to the story, fled the scene in a hurry.

The year before, in 1988, another encounter occurred between a real estate agent and a large creature with black, curly hair and what were described as inquisitive eyes. According to the story, residents in the area had complained that some kind of animal had been unsnapping the lids to their trash cans and rifling through their rubbish.

Bigfoot, the most popular cryptid of them all, is described as being similar to the yeti, yowie and other such creatures, in that it's often described as being covered in fur and quite large. Witnesses portray the creature as walking upright, while others describe a creature that uses all four limbs in a fashion like great primates. Their fur has been described as a dark, brownish red to a lighter, almost blonde color.

What draws these creatures to Sedona and other parts of the state? There are several theories that tackle this very question. While Sedona is heavily hiked and visitors pour into the community every day of the week, there are also rugged areas that are hard for mere humans to explore. This, combined with dense vegetation in particular locations, offers enough cover for wildlife, including bigfoot, to move around unseen. Another theory holds that the area's vortexes bring the creatures to the area. Like with any spiritual creature, the allure of the energies at play in Sedona are simply too much for these cryptids to resist. Still others believe the energy vortexes serve as portals that bigfoot has made use of to travel from one part of the Earth to another. This makes them similar to the portals alleged to exist at the Grand Canyon and in Upper Antelope Canyon.

Sedona may very well provide the resources needed for a bigfoot family to survive, including access to creeks and streams. They are largely believed to be omnivores, feeding on berries, plants, nuts, bugs and only the occasional small animal. There have also been reports of bigfoot indulging in larger

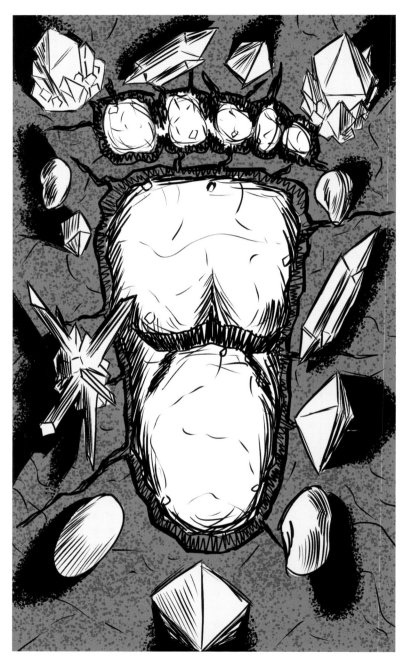

Bigfoot sightings, or the discovery of their prints, while not as common here as they are in the Pacific Northwest, are a regular occurrence in the Verde Valley, particularly in Sedona and the village of Oak Creek. *Illustration by Jason McLean.*

prey, such as elk. And all of this can be found in the Sedona region. Caves are also included in the area's geography, and it is commonly believed bigfoot regularly make use of cave systems for both shelter and secrecy.

Some theories have tried to explain the existence of bigfoot through scientific means. Using eyewitness descriptions, alleged physical evidence and Native legends, scientists have tried to piece together a better understanding of the giant and elusive creature. Cryptid experts think there may be an undiscovered ape offshoot that would explain the existence of the creature, possibly a primate distantly related to orangutans or gorillas. The creature's often-described low brow, "caveman-like" head and long arms would lead one to believe they are indeed related to apes, and proponents of the theory insist they are. Still others theorize that it may be a surviving species of a prehistoric hominid, such as gigantopithecus. Deniers, however, point out a lack of skeletal remains or any DNA at all as proof that bigfoot, as well as many other legendary cryptids, are anything other than a part of cultural folklore.

Cryptid historians point out the term *bigfoot* is relatively new in relation to the creature. As previously mentioned, the creature was originally called sasquatch. The "bigfoot" moniker is said to have been adopted in the 1950s during a rush of alleged sightings in Northern California, which is where one of the world's most well-known sightings occurred. It was even captured on film: the notorious Patterson-Gimlin film shot in 1967. The footage shows what bigfoot fans believed at the time to be a female of the species.

The sixteen-millimeter film footage was recorded in October 1967 by Roger Patterson and Robert Gimlin. Shot in Bluff Creek, California, the footage depicts a large, hairy creature walking along a dry creek bed in broad daylight. Patterson and Gimlin were on a horseback expedition seeking evidence of bigfoot when they spotted the creature. Patterson, it's said, dismounted his horse and began filming. The creature appeared for a total of sixteen seconds. In the footage, which shows a creature with swinging arms, the bigfoot, later nicknamed Patty, turns and looks at the camera before disappearing from into the forest.

The footage kicked off a media firestorm that supercharged interest in the bigfoot legend during that time, though several viewers questioned its authenticity. Skeptics claim the creature was merely someone dressed in a gorilla suit and that the film was staged for the profit such documentation would earn. Others believe the footage is real and insist the movements, such as the swinging arms, couldn't be faked by someone in a suit or through practical effects, as computer-generated imagery (CGI) didn't exist back then in the way it does today.

Of course, interest in bigfoot already existed, thanks to a handful of other isolated encounters. Prior to the Patterson-Gimlin film, the Ape Canyon incident of 1924 is one of the more famous encounters that occurred in the Pacific Northwest. The incident occurred in July that year when a clutch of miners reported being violently attacked in Ape Canyon, near Mount Saint Helens in Washington State.

Other famous bigfoot encounters include an incident that occurred in August 2010. Hunter Justin Smeja came forward with the wild claim he had shot and killed two hairy beasts in the Sierra Nevada Mountains of California, though he was later charged with a variety of crimes, including lying under oath. Then there's the Lake Worth Monster of Lake Worth Texas, where, in 1969, multiple eyewitness accounts described a giant hairy creature behaving belligerently. According to witnesses, the creature threw tires and rocks toward those who were getting too close. Another famed creature, also often connected with the bigfoot legends, is the inspiration behind the classic B film *The Legend of Boggy Creek*. The Foukes Monster was first sighted in May 1971 by hunter Bobby Ford, who described it as a lumbering ape-like creature.

Some have even tried to apprehend the creature, such as the group of men who, in 1974, built a bigfoot trap in Siskiyou County, California. They erected a large steel cage and filled it with delectables, fruit and meat in the hopes it would lure the elusive creature. Their attempts, unsurprisingly, were not met with success. They never did catch a bigfoot.

While Arizona may not be synonymous with bigfoot encounters, residents here have had their fair share. The Mogollon Monster, featured in chapter 15, is one of the state's most famous bigfoot legends, while others think the two creatures are distinctly separate species. From desert landscapes to the higher, forested elevations, Arizona has accommodations for the elusive, furry sasquatch no matter the temperature.

Sightings have been reported in the Apache-Sitgreaves National Forest, located in the eastern portion of the state, and made famous by the UFO abduction of Travis Walton, covered in chapter 12. Over the years, witnesses there have described creatures similar to those from other reports: a hairy bipedal (two-legged creature) making its way silently through the forest. There have even been reports of vocalization. The White Mountains, found within the Apache-Sitgreaves region, have hosted a handful of sightings. Witnesses there report tall, hairy beasts crossing rugged country roads, peeking into cabin windows after dark and loitering in the foliage near campsites. Some have even claimed the creatures are responsible for missing livestock and pets in this area. One such incident occurred on July 14, 2020, around 11:30 p.m., as a man drove home along Forest Road 249 from the Big Lake Recreation Area. According to the man's testimony, a large bipedal creature stepped out into the road about one hundred feet in front of him. By his estimation, the creature, which turned and faced him before running into the wilderness, weighed upward of four hundred pounds.

Not all members of the bigfoot family prefer forests and cooler temperatures, however, as there have been reported encounters in the desert portions of the state. Bigfoot sightings have been reported in the Sonoran Desert; there, it has been seen crossing dry washes and making its way through rocky canyons. Near Phoenix, in the White Tank area, an encounter occurred somewhere between 1993 and 1994 to three high school kids late one night. After hearing a commotion in the bushes outside their vehicles, the boys grabbed their flashlights and got out of the vehicle. Within moments, they found themselves face to face with a creature that stood on two legs; they said it was at least eight feet tall with tan and brown hair. Upon being discovered, the creature quickly made its way deep into the shrubbery and vanished into the desert.

In 2015, Arizona Department of Transportation officials posted to their Facebook page an image believers claim proves the existence of bigfoot in northern Arizona. In the snowy image, which shows State Route 260 near Heber, several dark shapes are seen foraging along the side of the road. Despite the blurriness of the image, the post went viral and generated thousands of comments. The caption for the photograph reads, "We might have spotted a family of Sasquatches on SR 260 near Heber this afternoon. What do you think?"

While certain witnesses have come forward with stories of encounters with these giants of the forest, they aren't always the most reliable sources. Many have faked their way to notoriety by fabricating evidence of bigfoot confrontations.

Two of the more notable hoaxes perpetrated on unsuspecting believers include the 2008 discovery of a sasquatch corpse in Georgia. The incident occurred in 2008 in northern Georgia, where two men filled a costume with animal guts and passed it off, through videos and photographs, as a dead bigfoot. They originally claimed they discovered the corpse while hiking, though the discovery was quickly revealed to be a fake. Perhaps the biggest hoax was that of the Piltdown Man, originally reported in 1912 in England. Said to be the missing link between humans and apes, the discovery looked like the skull of a sasquatch, at least until the truth came out. The skull was, in fact, a human skull with the jawbone of an orangutan attached to it.

18

PHOENIX

Chilling Chupacabra Tales

There are stories of bloodsuckers in every culture across the globe. But most think of a particular cryptid when they hear those two words. They think of a dapper gentleman with black hair that creates a widow's peak above a set of beckoning, dark eyes, a velvet cloak and red jewel at his neck, with a drop of blood lovingly smeared on one side of his lower lip, just above a set of menacing fangs. We think of vampires portrayed by Bela Lugosi, Christopher Lee and even Gary Oldman. There are, however, other bloodsuckers at large in the world, creatures that are less sensual than vampires, creatures like the Slavic legends of the strigois, believed to be undead humans with flaming-red hair, two hearts and the ability to turn into other animals (similar to the legend of the skinwalkers). They are sometimes associated with vampirism, as they need blood to survive and certainly fall into the bloodsucking cryptid category. A lesser-known bloodsucker is the Arkansas snipe, also known as the skeeteroo, which, as its name implies, is a giant insect with a penchant for doing what all mosquitoes do: drinking blood. The skeeteroo was made popular by the trading card game *Metazoo: Cryptid Nation*. Other bloodsucking cryptids include the aswang from Filipino culture, the leak witch from Indonesia, the wakwak vampire bird from Philippine mythology and, of course, the ferocious chupacabra.

The chupacabra, formally known as el chupacabra, is firmly entrenched in the category of bloodsucking cryptids. In fact, the creature is named for that very attribute. It's known as the "goat sucker" (*chupacabra* in Spanish) for its chilling ability to drain every drop of blood from the goats and

El Chupacabra is a popular cryptid of the American Southwest and beyond. *Chupacabra*, in English, roughly translates to "goat sucker." Like vampires, they're known for drinking the blood of their victims. *Illustration by Paul Van de Carr.*

cattle it typically preys upon. Thought to be the size of an average dog, the chupacabra is widely known for its hulking fangs, larger and fiercer than Bela Lugosi's fangs, and a pair of glowing red eyes.

For decades, stories of the chupacabra have struck terror in the hearts and minds of Arizona residents, with sightings reported throughout the southwest. Of course, the modern chupacabra tales spring from Puerto Rico, where sightings of the wild, horrible beast have circulated since the 1980s. Stories and chupacabra sightings have proliferated over the years. Sightings have been reported throughout the American Southwest and into Latin America. Eyewitnesses have reported having chupacabra encounters in all corners of the state of Arizona.

The beast, not terribly large, is often reported as walking on its hind legs like a human. Some claim the creature hops around, as nimble as a kangaroo, while its ruby-red eyes seek out new victims. Others claim it walks on all four legs. Some claim the animal has no fur but is instead covered in scales like a lizard. Its spine, many witnesses say, is covered in spikes, making it a fierce addition to the hefty cryptid encyclopedia. Over the years, farmers claimed it was a chupacabra, not anything else, responsible for the grisly mutilation of their farm animals, particularly when those corpses appear drained of blood with precision cuts visible on their lifeless bodies. There are those who claim they have seen flying chupacabras as well.

When it comes to farm animals, of course, there can be many reasons death can occur, and most mysterious deaths can be solved using science. For instance, cuts that appear to be made with keen incisions are more likely to have been caused by gas buildup within the animal's body. When those gases erupt, they split the skin in a manner that makes it appear cut by a surgical incision.

Nonetheless, theories abound when it comes to the chupacabra. Some claim they're simply injured animals suffering from mange, a skin disease caused by microscopic mites. Two types of mange are most associated with chupacabra sightings: demodectic (a contagious form of mange) and sarcoptic mange, which can be an indicator of parvo or distemper. Still others claim the dog-like terrors are the descendants of pets left behind by visiting aliens. Like most pets and their caretakers, these animals need to be taken out for walks and bathroom breaks periodically. As will occasionally happen, one or two always manage to escape. In this theory, those escaped alien pets were left behind and managed to survive and reproduce. Still others think the beasts are a form of ape or even marsupials, carnivorous descendants of the kangaroo.

But stories of the chupacabra die hard. Its presence has been reported outside of the Southwest, where it's known as the "bigfoot of Latino culture." The Appalachian chupacabra, for instance, is said to be four feet tall at the shoulder with spikes along its back and a pig-like snout. Common belief is that the Appalachian chupacabra migrated from Puerto Rico to the Appalachian Mountains.

There have been numerous reports of the original Puerto Rican creatures. Originally, the chupacabra was said to resemble a monstrous gargoyle, but as the sightings spread to other parts of the world, including Arizona, the descriptions began to change as well from a menacing gargoyle to a dog-like creature with three toes. A famous account from the mid-1990s blamed the chupacabra for the deaths of a handful of sheep, all found drained of blood with corresponding teeth marks on their bodies. Not long thereafter, an even deadlier attack occurred in which turkeys, rabbits, horses, cats, dogs and cattle were all found dead and drained of blood on a Puerto Rican farm. The year 1995 was a pivotal moment in the lore of the chupacabra, as a total of one thousand Puerto Rican animal deaths were blamed on the bloodthirsty cryptid. At one or two of these sites, three-toed animal prints were reported, and many residents offered eyewitness accounts.

In 2008, police cameras in DeWitt County, Texas, captured what witnesses believe to be footage of a local chupacabra. The animal in the video can be seen running along the side of the road under a bright sun; it is grayish in appearance and shows off two pointed ears. Experts have speculated that the furless animal pictured isn't a chupacabra at all but a coyote or canine badly infected with a skin condition.

Over the years, Texas officials have evaluated numerous carcasses thought to be deceased chupacabras, only to determine the animals were part coyote with, oddly enough, legs longer than typical coyote legs. Their snouts, too, were longer than what is normally associated with a coyote. Lower fangs were also reported on the carcasses, according to a 2012 *Tucson Weekly* article.

In February 2013, an Oklahoma man photographed what he believed to be a chupacabra standing in the middle of a field. The picture, taken during daylight hours, shows a scraggly, hairless creature lurking among the brown brambles. The man, Craig Martin, said the first thing that popped into head as he took the beast's photograph was that he had captured on camera the legendary chupacabra. Martin also said the creature feasted on the remains of a dead animal in the field. In the same KFOR-TV news story, however, a spokesperson for the Oklahoma Department of Wildlife said he believed the animal was the result of a coyote breeding with another animal, likely a dog. It might also be suffering from mange, he added.

Later that year, in October 2013, a resident of Picayune, Mississippi, reported their own sighting of a chupacabra. One family, who was returning home from a boating trip, described the creature: "If a zombie had a dog, it would look like that." Other eyewitness accounts described the creature as a "squatch dog," or bigfoot dog.

In Arizona, there have been many chupacabra sightings, and witnesses have posted numerous photographs across social media showing the creature they allegedly encountered. One such encounter was posted to Facebook in July 2016. Bradley Kreis of Sun City posted possible chupacabra photographs to his page. A year later, in 2017, KOLD News 13 in Tucson posted to its Facebook page an image of what appeared to be a coyote with mange. The image, taken by Mario Robles in February that year, shows the animal on

In 1995, one thousand animal deaths were blamed on the chupacabra in Puerto Rico. Many of those animals were found drained of blood. *Illustration by Jason McLean.*

Thirty-Sixth Street, near the community's railroad tracks, with the question, "What do you think it is?" While Sedona is more commonly associated with sightings of UFOs, vortexes and bigfoot (see the chapter 17), residents there have reported encounters with chupacabra as well. One notable sighting occurred in red rock country, where a Sedona resident allegedly encountered a dog-like creature with glowing red eyes near their property.

Meteorologist Erin Christensen also reported a Tucson chupacabra sighting in 2012, when she reported a creature passing in front of the headlights of her car on Speedway Boulevard. *Tucson Weekly* columnist Ryn Gargulinski wrote that her own fiancé observed a variation of the typical chupacabra while sitting in his pickup truck on Houghton Road. He reported a bear-like creature with a head like a cow walking on two legs.

Tombstone is home to one of the earliest chupacabra incidents on record, dating to April 1890, though some question whether the creature was another form of cryptid, perhaps a prehistoric bird, as the flying creature's wingspan was estimated to be 160 feet, and its body measured almost 90 feet, which would make it the largest chupacabra yet. Even if it isn't, the story is worth including. Two cowboys were said to have seen the large bird, which they said had the face of an alligator, and then they followed it first on horseback and then on foot before they allegedly shot and killed it. The story of the giant bird, or winged chupacabra, appeared in the Tombstone newspaper, the *Epitaph*. And an accompanying photograph titled "Thunderbird" has populated internet sites; it shows a group of six men standing over the giant bird's remains.

In 2015, a viewer from Surprise posted an alleged chupacabra photograph to the 12 News Facebook page. The image shows a canine-like creature walking along the side of the road, though many believe that sighting was also of a coyote suffering from hair loss due to a skin disease.

The creatures are now celebrated throughout pop culture, from animated children's movies to horror films. Books cover the subject extensively as well, from the nonfiction title *Tracking the Chupacabra: The Vampire Beast in Fact, Fiction, and Folklore*, by Benjamin Radford, to the children's book *The Chupacabra Ate the Candelabra*, by Marc Tyler Nobleman and Ana Aranda.

Despite the chupacabra's popularity, encountering one in the dead of night isn't recommended. The same can be said for our next—and final—cryptid, La Llorona.

Tucson and Other Areas

Stories of La Llorona

Stories of La Llorona, or the weeping woman, are told in hushed whispers among the children of the Southwest and shared loudly by adults who hope to frighten good behavior into their offspring. Believers claim that simply touching the La Llorona will leave you burned. No matter what form the legend takes, whether the woman is dressed in white or all black, the stories always carry a sense of dread with them. She's been called a variety of names, from the "Ditch Witch" or the "Cryer" to the "Wailing Woman," the "Crying Woman" and everything in between. In Latino culture, La Llorona is a well-known legend that has spread throughout the southwestern states. In Arizona, there are stories of La Llorona from Tucson to the Grand Canyon, including the wailing woman of the Santa Fe Dam in Williams and the crying woman of the Santa Cruz River in Tucson. It's rumored she appears near any large body of water, from wells and ditches to rivers and lakes, always seeking more children to drown.

The spectral apparition is described as wearing a sopping wet gown covered in blackish mud. Her stringy hair often hangs over her dark eyes, dripping wet and fouled with muck. Others say she wears a shroud or wedding veil over her face. Still others have claimed they saw the bones of dead children on her back or indicated she appeared as an attractive, dark-haired beauty. Storytellers who have shared tales of the crying woman say they've heard her wails of sorrow from a distance and encountered her when they've moved closer to investigate. Her wails are often described as a lure,

Descriptions of the Wailing Woman, or La Llorona, vary. She's been observed dressed in a white gown by the Santa Fe Dam south of Williams. *Illustration by Paul Van de Carr.*

bringing those curious enough to investigate to their sudden death. Some claim the spectral visitor can be called forth during a séance, while others insist she comes only to misbehaving children or lone travelers who have strayed too close to the edge of a body of water.

La Llorona's origin story, which dates back hundreds of years, varies from region to region, even from one person to the next, with some claiming the ghostly woman drowned her children out of anger at an unfaithful husband. She was cursed to search for those drowned children for eternity as a result. Variations to that story claim she sought her children when her anger subsided and drowned while looking for their bodies. Another holds that it was La Llorona herself who was the promiscuous one. She drowned her children instead of being held accountable for them later. But when she died, the woman faced a reckoning in heaven. She'd have to locate her drowned children and bring them with her before she was allowed to enter the pearly gates.

Storyteller Tony Norris of Flagstaff shares the tale of a jilted woman named Maria. According to his account, she was a young girl who dreamed of marrying a handsome cowboy. Despite being warned that there were better attributes to be found in a partner, Maria married her cowboy. The two built a home together along the waterlogged banks of Flagstaff's Rio de Flag. Later, during monsoon season, the man showed up to inform Maria that he'd met another woman and wanted to see only his children. She was so angered that she hurled her children into the storm-fueled river, where they died. When she realized her egregious act, she ran along the river, hoping to save them, but instead tripped and hit her head on a rock. She was killed instantly.

A variation of the legend holds the doomed woman was a single mother of two who lived in poverty in a small village. According to the stories, this woman became smitten with a wealthy man. The man, however, didn't return her affections. When she pressed him for a reason, he informed her he wanted no children and pointed out that she had not one but two of them. Thinking only of her desire, she took her children to a nearby river and, during the darkest hours of the night, drowned them there. Now childless, she returned to the wealthy man and told him what she had done.

Yet another legend, one many in Tucson hold to be true, says that La Llorona hails from Nogales and moved to Tucson without her children. As bad luck would have it, rain caused the Santa Cruz River to flood shortly after, and the riverbanks spilled over, drowning her children, washing them upriver into the Tucson community.

The Santa Cruz River runs through Tucson in Pima County from its beginning in the San Rafael Valley. From there, it flows south into Mexico but takes a U turn and then runs north through the Tohono O'odham Nation, right through Tucson and into Marana. It's said the river has been a part of the land for thousands of years and has had its difficulties during this time. Human habitation has dried the river and even altered its course. Parts of the river, due to excessive pumping, remain dry to this day, only filling when it rains. In recent years, efforts have begun to restore the river to its former self. With effluent water treated in Pima County facilities, the river is beginning to reappear along a twenty-mile section by Tucson near Marana. In fact, 2017 saw the return of the Gila Topminnow, which, for years, had not been seen, though it is now closer to Nogales, which is also releasing treated effluent. It's the Santa Cruz River that attracted Tucson's first residents over twelve thousand years ago, as they were drawn to the natural water source and the animals and riparian habitat that came with it

The river's return to vitality may also mean the return of the La Llorona—if she's ever truly left. There have been many tales of a crying woman along the river in the years after her children are alleged to have drowned there.

Accounts of her appearances are legion, including a 1968 story by folklore writer Bess Lomax Hawes, which shared an incident in which La Llorona appeared in a juvenile detention building in California.

In Arizona, sightings of the wailing woman have been reported in Tucson from the South Stone Avenue underpass to the aforementioned Santa Cruz Riverbanks and all the way to the Grand Canyon and Williams, where stories of a wailing woman have been reported at the Santa Fe Dam. In one alleged instance, a police officer on patrol near the dam heard a woman sobbing. He called his report in and proceeded to wander the shore of the dam with his flashlight. While the sobbing continued, he could never find the woman herself.

In Maricopa, journalist Michelle Chance reported in 2018 an old tale involving Vice-Mayor Brent Murphree. The city of Maricopa is located in Pinal County in the Gila River Valley. With a population of more than sixty-six thousand as of 2022, it ranks as Pinal County's largest incorporated municipality. Murphree's encounter with La Llorona occurred in the summer of 1974, when he and a group of other teens returned from church camp. During a stormy evening, Murphree rode with his mother as she dropped off campers. During a stop at the Headquarters Café, according to the *In Maricopa* story, Murphree spotted two friends inside, and he convinced his

Some describe La Llorona as a waterlogged woman wearing a veil, constantly searching bodies of water for the children she drowned herself. *Illustration by Jason McLean.*

mother to go on without him. After his dinner with friends, they all set out into the rainy night. They drove east on Honeycutt Road, down into an unlit wash along a dirt road surrounded by pecan groves. The wash was already filling with water from the steady, unrelenting monsoon. As they neared the top on the other side, they saw a woman dressed in white standing nearby. She was drenched from head to toe, Murphree recalled. Thinking she might be lost, Murphree said he nearly got out of the vehicle to help. His friends, who knew the story of La Llorona, refused to let the fourteen-year-old out of the car and instead sped up to flee the area. Murphree described the woman as being fair-haired with an eerie, blank stare. Ever since, he said, he's had an interest in tales of La Llorona.

Christopher Rodarte, the author of the book *La Llorona: Ghost Stories of the Southwest*, believes this particular ghost story may be the oldest to have come out of South America, Mexico and the southwestern United States. Novelist Rudolfo Anaya wrote of the famed cryptid in his 1984 book *The Legend of La Llorona*. In it, he wrote she was an enslaved Indigenous woman forced to be the interpreter and concubine of a conquistador.

The legend's popularity reached a boiling point in 2019 with the release of the film *The Curse of La Llorona*, starring Linda Cardellini, Raymond Cruz, Patricia Velasquez and Marisol Ramirez as the wailing woman herself. The film, directed by Michael Chaves, was released in April 2019 and was shot in Los Angeles, California. The one-hour-and-thirty-three-minute New Line Cinema movie cost an estimated $9 million in all to produce and earned more than $54 million in the United States and Canada alone, proving that interest in the legend of La Llorona remains high. *The Legend of La Llorona* followed in 2022, starring actor Danny Trejo.

BIBLIOGRAPHY

All That's Interesting. "Inside the Chupacabra Legend and Its Stories of Blood-Sucking Terror." www.allthatsinteresting.com/chupacabra.

———. "Inside the Gruesome Murder of Bob Crane, the *Hogan's Heroes* Star Who Was Beat to Death in 1978." www.allthatsinteresting.com/bob-crane-death.

———. "Meet the Navajo Skinwalker, the Demonic Shapeshifter That Native Americans Won't Even Mention by Name." www.allthatsinteresting.com/skinwalker.

ASU Grand Canyon Conservancy. "Hyde River Tragedy." www.grcahistory.org/sites/colorado-river-corridor/hyde-river-tragedy/.

AZ Central. "Arizona Has 4th Most UFO Sightings in the US. See the Rankings." www.azcentral.com/story/news/local/arizona/2024/02/17/arizona-ufo-sightings/72612486007/.

———. "Forget Bigfoot. Arizona Locals Know to Watch Out for the Mogollon Monster." www.azcentral.com/story/entertainment/life/2023/08/18/what-is-mogollon-monster-arizona-cryptid/70606467007/.

———. "*Hogan's Heroes* Star Bob Crane Was Murdered 40 Years Ago. Why Does It Still Fascinate Us?" www.azcentral.com/story/news/local/arizona-best-reads/2018/06/29/hogans-heroes-star-bob-crane-scottsdale-murder-40-years-later/733260002/.

———. "What Were the Phoenix Lights? Why The UFO Phenomenon Is Still a Mystery 27 Years Later." www.azcentral.com/story/entertainment/life/2024/03/13/phoenix-lights-ufo-history/72630635007/.

Bigfootencounters.com. "Sedona, Arizona Summer 1989." www.bigfootencounters.com/sbs/sedona.htm.

Branning, Debe. *Haunted Phoenix*. Charleston, SC: The History Press, 2018.

Dangerous Roads. "Travelling through the Haunted Route 666, the Devil's Highway." www.dangerousroads.org/north-america/usa/4993-route-666.html.

Davis-Monthan Air Force Base. "About DM." www.dm.af.mil/About-DM/Units/355th-Fighter-Group/.

Dennett, Preston. *UFOs Over Arizona: A True History of Extraterrestrial Encounters in the Grand Canyon State.* Atglen, PA: Schiffer Publishing, 2016.

Distractify. "Alien Abductee Travis Walton Opens Up in a New Doc: 'The Terror I Experienced Might Not Have Been Warranted' (EXCLUSIVE)." www.distractify. com/p/travis-walton-alien-abduction.

Entertainment Weekly. "The Tragic, Unsolved Murder of *Hogan's Heroes* Star Bob Crane." www.ew.com/tv/2019/08/26/bob-crane-hogans-heroes-unsolved-murder/.

Eppinga, Jane. *Tucson, Arizona.* Images of America. Charleston, SC: Arcadia Publishing, 2000.

Federal Bureau of Investigation (FBI). "John Dillinger." www.fbi.gov/history/ famous-cases/john-dillinger.

Forever AZ. "Haunted History of the Bird Cage Theatre in Tombstone, AZ." www. foreveraz.com/haunted-history-bird-cage-theatre/.

Gardner, Renée. *Southern Arizona's Most Haunted.* Atglen, PA: Schiffer Publishing, 2010.

Geographical Cure. "Guide to the Vortexes of Sedona Arizona for Non-Believers." www.thegeographicalcure.com/post/vortexes-of-sedona.

Ghiglieri, Michael P., and Thomas M. Myers. *Over the Edge: Death in Grand Canyon.* 2nd ed. Grand Canyon, AZ: Puma Press, 2012.

Grunge. "Kurt Russell Reported the Famed Phoenix Lights UFO Sighting." www. grunge.com/867318/kurt-russell-reported-the-famed-phoenix-lights-ufo-sighting/.

Harper, Renee. *Paranormal Arizona.* Atglen, PA: Schiffer Publishing, 2018.

Haunted Places. "El Tovar Hotel." www.hauntedplaces.org/item/el-tovar-hotel/.

HauntedUS.com. "Bird Cage Theatre's Paranormal Claims." www.hauntedus.com/ arizona/bird-cage-theatre/.

Heidinger, Lisa Schnebly, Janeen Trevillyan and the Sedona Historical Society. *Sedona.* Images of America. Charleston, SC: Arcadia Publishing, 2007.

Hendersen, Frank. *Bigfoot in Arizona: Mysterious Encounters.* N.p.: self-published, 2023.

Historic Hotels of America. "Discover El Tovar Hotel, Which Is the Premier Lodging Facility at the Grand Canyon National Park Where President Theodore Roosevelt Stayed." www.historichotels.org/us/hotels-resorts/el-tovar-hotel/history.php.

Jacobson, Patricia, and Midge Steuber. *Haunted Jerome.* Charleston, SC: The History Press, 2019.

Johnson, Susan. *Haunted Flagstaff.* Charleston, SC: The History Press, 2022.

KGUN 9. "A Different Type of Chill: Touring Haunted Hotel Congress." www. kgun9.com/news/local-news/downtown-tucson-news/a-different-type-of-chill-touring-haunted-hotel-congress.

Leatherman, Benjamin. "The Phoenix Lights UFO Sightings in 1997: An Oral History." *Phoenix New Times*, March 10, 2022. www.phoenixnewtimes. com/arts/the-phoenix-lights-ufo-sightings-in-1997-an-oral-history-25th-anniversary-13176244.

Legends of America. "Haunted Monte Vista Hotel in Flagstaff, Arizona." www. legendsofamerica.com/az-montevista/.

———. "Navajo Skinwalkers—Witches of the Southwest." www.legendsofamerica. com/navajo-skinwalkers/.

Mallett, Daryl F. *Haunted Tucson.* Charleston, SC: The History Press, 2023.

Mental Floss. "An Empty Boat in the Grand Canyon: The Mysterious Disappearance of Glen and Bessie Hyde." www.mentalfloss.com/posts/glen-bessie-hyde-grand-canyon-disappearance.

Mountain Tripper. "Hotel Monte Vista." www.mountaintripper.com/historic-buildings-arizona/hotel-monte-vista/.

North American Cryptids. "The Mogollon Monster: Arizona's Mysterious Bigfoot." www.northamericancryptids.com/mogollon-monster/.

Norton, Clark. *Secret Tucson: A Guide to the Weird, Wonderful, and Obscure.* St. Louis, MO: Reedy Press, 2019.

O.K. Corral. "A Brief History of the Famous Gunfight at the O.K. Corral." www.ok-corral.com/pages/history.shtml.

Only in Your State. "A Night at This Historic Arizona Hotel Will Feel Like You Stepped Back in Time." www.onlyinyourstate.com/arizona/az-historic-hotel/.

———. "This One-of-a-Kind Shrine Found in Arizona Has an Astounding History." www.onlyinyourstate.com/arizona/wishing-shrine-tucson-az/.

Phoenix Ghosts. "The Orpheum Theatre Phoenix." www.phoenixghosts.com/the-orpheum-theatre-phoenix/.

Phoenix Theater History. "Orpheum Theatre." www.phoenixtheaterhistory.com/companies/orpheum-theatre/.

Polston, Cody. *Haunted Tombstone.* Charleston, SC: The History Press, 2018.

Rodarte. *La Llorona: Ghost Stories of the Southwest.* Tucson, AZ: La Llorona Productions, 2019.

Sedona.net. "Sedona Vortex & Vortex Experiences." www.sedona.net/vortex.

Strange Outdoors. "The Strange Disappearance of Glen and Bessie Hyde from the Grand Canyon National Park." www.strangeoutdoors.com/mysterious-stories-blog/glen-bessie-hyde.

TheCinemaholic. "Travis Walton: Where Is Alleged Alien Abductee Now?" www.thecinemaholic.com/travis-walton-where-is-alleged-alien-abductee-now/.

Think Aboutits. "4,000 Year Old UFO Found in Grand Canyon—Article." www.thinkaboutitdocs.com/4000-year-old-ufo-found-in-grand-canyon/.

True West Magazine. "Tales of AZ Route 666: The Devil's Highway." www.truewestmagazine.com/route666/.

Tucson.com. "15 Out of This World Reports of UFOs Spotted Over Tucson." www.tucson.com/news/local/15-out-of-this-world-reports-of-ufos-spotted-over-tucson/article_d45118e2-801c-11e6-8147-77c991d947a0.html.

UFOmania. "Grand Canyon UFO Crash Site – The 4000 Year Old Secret." YouTube. May 20, 2018. www.youtube.com/watch?v=HtmaiaqKssg.

U.S. Department of Transportation. "U.S. 666: 'Beast of a Highway'?" www.highways.dot.gov/highway-history/general-highway-history/us-666-beast-highway.

Visit Tucson. "El Tiradito/The Wishing Shrine." www.visittucson.org/listing/el-tiradito-the-wishing-shrine/816/.

Weatherly, David. *Copper State Monsters: Cryptids & Legends of Arizona.* N.p.: Eerie Lights Publishing, 2019.

Weird U.S. "La Llorona—The Phantom Banshee." www.weirdus.com/states/arizona/local_legends/la_llorona_and_launa/index.php.

ABOUT THE AUTHOR

Patrick Whitehurst writes fiction and nonfiction, including six nonfiction books and four short fiction works. His short stories have appeared in *Punk Noir*, *Shotgun Honey*, *Pulp Modern*, *Hoosier Noir*, *Guilty Crime Story Flash*, *Mystery Tribune Flash* and *Switchblade* magazine. He's been featured in the anthologies *Bitter Chills*, *Shotgun Honey Presents: Recoil*, *Trouble in Tucson* and elsewhere. Find him online at www.patrickwhitehurst.com.